Christian Faith 101

Christian Faith 101

The Basics and Beyond

Steven Tsoukalas

Judson Press
Valley Forge

Christian Faith 101: The Basics and Beyond

© 2000 by Judson Press, Valley Forge, PA 19482-0851

Library of Congress Cataloging-in-Publication Data

Tsoukalas, Steven, 1956–
    Christian faith 101 : the basics and beyond / Steven Tsoukalas.
        p.   cm.
    Includes bibliographical references.
    ISBN 0-8170-1361-X (pbk. : alk. paper)
    1. Theology, Doctrinal. I. Title: Christian faith one hundred one.
II. Title: Christian faith one hundred one. III. Title.
BT77.T78   2000
230—dc21   00-021213

Printed in the U.S.A.

06 05 04

10 9 8 7 6 5 4 3

For my wife, Sandy,
who was used of the Lord
to inspire this project

CONTENTS

PREFACE

WHEN GOD SAVED ME BACK ON DECEMBER 15, 1983, HE DID SO by giving me that childlike faith in Christ as the only way of salvation and the only one in whom there is life. As a young man of twenty-seven years of age, I could not imagine anything more exciting.

Quickly afterward came the desire to learn more about the truths of God contained in the Bible. I wanted to learn more about the God of the universe and God's ways. I wanted to learn more about the "things of God." Yet even this was not of my own desire. It was a desire the Lord placed in my heart, a desire born from the Lord, who is gracious, patient, and glorified when God's children learn from God about God.

I believe that every Christian is given this desire. How could it be otherwise? God wants us to grow in knowledge of him. I hope and pray that this book will aid you in this.

—

First Things

THIS BOOK IS WRITTEN FOR THE LAYPERSON TO USE AS AN AID in knowing better the One who has brought eternal life.

How to Use This Book

Read this book with the Bible close by, for it is only a pointer to the gems the Bible contains. When a Bible verse is cited, try to read a bit before and a bit after the verse. A Bible that is sectioned off by paragraphs or section headings will make it easier for you to know where to start and where to end your reading.

This book can be quite useful in group settings, perhaps for a weekly study led by a facilitator who is adequately learned in **Christian doctrine.** In this setting, the discussion sections in each chapter will reinforce the chapter's content and stimulate further discussion and learning.

Basics and Beyond

Each chapter, except the last one, contains a "Basics" section and a "Beyond the Basics" section. This leaves you the option of reading only the "Basics" section, or both.

"The Basics" is designed to give you just that—the basics! "Beyond the Basics" is designed for those who want to be stretched a bit. This section has more advanced theological concepts, including transliterations of Greek and Hebrew words. Remember, however, that "Beyond the Basics" is still written for the layperson! Additionally, "Beyond the Basics" serves as a primer for those who later may desire further formal theological study.

Discussion Sections

At the end of each "Basics" and "Beyond the Basics" section are sections that contain questions and suggestions for discussion, aimed especially at discussion groups. In some cases the answers are obvious, while other questions and discussion themes are designed to allow the group to probe beyond what is written in this book. Again, the discussion sections are designed to reinforce the chapter's content and stimulate further discussion and learning.

Meditations

Each chapter concludes with a "Meditation" section. I believe that studying the things of God **(theology)** should lead to expression in life. Both study and expression are what I term "doing theology." In turn, doing theology is also worship. Many activities constitute worship. Studying about God is worship, as is expressing what is learned about God and going through our daily activities in acknowledgment of God's presence and grace.

Glossary

There is a glossary at the end of this book. When a word found in the glossary is used in the text, it will appear in **bold letters.** Bold lettering will occur in the first instance of the word in each chapter. With the exception of **redemption**, note that words that have their own sections (such as "adoption") will not be listed in the glossary. Finally, I have included in the glossary some words that are not found in the text, such as **interpretation** and **hermeneutics,** to aid those who may desire to pursue more advanced studies.

Suggested Readings

Also found at the end of the book is a brief list of selected resources that might be helpful to you if you are interested in reading more about a particular doctrine or concept discussed in this book. This list is by no means comprehensive, but it does suggest a handful of texts that are accessible to the interested layperson.

Pronunciation Guide

Following is a guide to the pronunciation of transliterated Greek and Hebrew words. Transliteration allows Greek and Hebrew words to be written in English, enabling you to pronounce these words without reading the actual languages. There are a few vowels and vowel combinations you should note:

Vowel	Pronunciation
$\bar{e}$	$\bar{a}$ as in *play*
e	as in *let*
$\bar{o}$	as *oh*
o	as in *loss*
$o\bar{o}$	as *awe-oh*
i at the end of a word	$\bar{e}$ as in *Pete*
i within a word	as in *is*
ai	as *eye*
ei	$\bar{a}$ as in *play*
au	**ow** as in *cow*

The rest is as simple as reading English!

The Importance of Theology

"Know what you believe and why you believe it!" Have you heard that line before? Perhaps you heard it voiced by a preacher or perhaps by a friend. What was your reaction? I for one gave a resounding "Amen!"

What Is a Christian?

A Christian is someone who believes (trusts) in the biblical Christ and his sacrifice on the cross for sin. "The disciples were first called Christians in Antioch" (Acts 11:26). Thus disciples are Christians, and Christians are disciples, the basic meaning of which is "learner." Thus we might say that Christians are learners of the "apostles' teaching" (Acts 2:42). The word "Christian" may also be used as an adjective, as in the phrase "Christian doctrine."

Defending the Faith

I was just beginning the lifelong process of studying the things of God when I was challenged to study the Scriptures. "Always being ready to make a defense to everyone who asks you to give an account for the hope that is in you" (1 Peter 3:15), said the speaker. I found out later that the word "defense" was used in other contexts in Peter's time. One such use was the court, where the accused was allowed a time to "make a defense" before those assembled.

Written in the context of the persecution of Christians, Peter's words speak to us today. Of course there are varying degrees of persecution, but whenever Christians are actively engaged in sharing their faith, they will be called to make a defense, to engage in **apologetics,** regarding *what* they believe and *why* they believe it. This book is written to aid you in that task.

But More Importantly

Though defending the faith is important, I consider it secondary compared to knowing the things of God, putting that knowledge in the heart, and rendering to God glory by expressing that knowledge in worship and lifestyle. This, I am convinced, is the goal of theology. We read in Scripture that the early Christians "were continually devoting themselves to the apostles' teaching and to the fellowship, to the breaking of bread and to prayer" (Acts 2:42). They were *doing* theology. Again, doing theology involves studying about God and expressing in our lives what we learn.

God calls us to love him with all our heart, soul, mind, and strength (Mark 12:30). Many Christians forget the "mind" part of this command. As a result we see much apathy in the Church when it comes to studying the things of God. But nothing is at times more crucial than this aspect of the Christian life. After all, we were saved because someone gave us theology in the form of the gospel!

The Place of Theology

Doing theology must not be trivialized because it is a characteristic of the people of God. Learning more about God and expressing that knowledge in our lives also cultivates the already existing relationship we have with him. Can anything in our lives be more important than that (Mark 12:30)?

Theology Learned and Expressed Individually

We do theology individually, privately. One day when spring was becoming quite evident in New England, I took a walk down to the brook at the back of our property. I sat down on the soft brown grass. The water was flowing high over the small stone waterfall that reaches from one side to the other. The sky was clear and brilliantly blue, and I heard nothing but the quiet swirl of fresh water. I then recalled the teaching of Scripture about how the triune God created the heavens and the earth. Immediately, that knowledge turned into praise as my eyes passed back and forth between the brook and its surrounding woods to the blue sky above. This is what theology is about.

Theology Learned and Expressed in Church

We read in the book of Acts that the "three thousand souls" who were added to the Church devoted themselves to study and to fellowship (Acts 2:41–42). They met together to study and discuss what they learned. The writer of Hebrews encourages Christians not to abandon the practice of "assembling together, as is the habit of some" (Hebrews 10:25).

A vital part of doing theology (learning and expression) takes place within the community of faith—the church. This, of course, implies that the church to which we belong must teach sound doctrine. Such teaching should be the first issue addressed in any church search. If a church holds to Christian **orthodoxy,** we can then explore the possibility of attending regularly.

Christian Theology as a "Garment"

Doctrines are closely connected to one another. View them collectively as a piece of clothing. If one doctrine is denied or is off base in the slightest, the whole garment eventually suffers from the tear. For example, what if one were to deny the deity of Christ (that is, that Jesus is God the Son)? This person ends up denying the Christian doctrine of the Trinity (see chap. 1). Further, and as we shall see in chapter 2, the doctrine that Jesus is God the Son is closely tied to his being "unique" (or "only begotten"; see John 1:14). Thus, this same person ends up denying that Jesus is God's *only way* of salvation.

Essential and Nonessential Theology

In a sense, all theology is essential because it is found in the Bible. But some doctrines are so essential that to deny them would place one outside the Christian Church. In other words, with these doctrines there can be no disagreement within the Christian camp. Doctrines such as the Trinity, the deity and humanity of Christ, the deity and personality of the Holy Spirit, salvation by grace through faith in Christ alone, and Christ's bodily resurrection cannot be denied if the Church is to remain the Church. However, there are doctrines with which Christians can disagree. For example, in baptism do you sprinkle, pour, or immerse? Do you use wine or grape juice when celebrating the Lord's Supper?

How do we straddle the line between the essential and nonessential doctrines? A good rule to follow is the old adage: In essentials, unity; in nonessentials, charity. In other words, we should be unified in the theological essentials and tolerant regarding our varying beliefs about the nonessentials. In this book I shall present the essential doctrines and note differing views on some of the nonessential ones.

The Bible

Christians believe that the Bible is the Word of God. Each writer of the sixty-six books that make up the Old and New Testaments was inspired by the Holy Spirit to bring us God's original Word. But this was not done through dictation. God used the personalities and the life events of each author, as "men moved by the Holy Spirit spoke from God" (2 Peter 1:21). In this sense we can view the Bible as "word and flesh"—coming from God and through God's chosen instruments, *through* whom the Spirit spoke. We must, then, take the Bible as our rule and guide for faith and practice.

With the Bible as our guide, let's begin *doing* theology!

PART ONE

God

1

The Trinity and God the Father

NO OTHER ESSENTIAL **DOCTRINE** OF THE **CHRISTIAN** FAITH HAS been more misunderstood than the doctrine of the Trinity. It also has been virulently attacked throughout the centuries. The doctrine has, however, stood against attacks because it is thoroughly biblical.

The Basics

The word "Trinity" is a combination of two words—*tri* and *unity*. There are three basic concepts to remember: (1) there is one eternal God; (2) God is the Father and the Son (Jesus) and the Holy Spirit; (3) the Father, the Son, and the Holy Spirit are three distinct **persons** who exist at the same time.

Now let's take our three basic concepts separately.

One God

As a Christian, you are a **monotheist;** that is, you are one who believes in only one God. But since some believe in one God *among others,* the Christian must expand the definition to mean that in reality only one God exists. This is biblical. The apostle

Paul states that any other gods are "so-called gods" (1 Corinthians 8:5) and that these so-called gods "by nature are no gods" (Galatians 4:8). Paul is in line with the prophet Isaiah, through whom God said, "Before Me there was no God formed, / and there will be none after Me" (Isaiah 43:10).

Father, Son, and Holy Spirit

We believe that the triune God is the Father and the Son and the Holy Spirit (see Matthew 28:19). We will study the three parts of this statement individually.

God is the Father. There is a person called "the Father" who is also called "God." In 2 Peter 1:17 we read, "For . . . He [Jesus] received honor and glory from God the Father."

And the Son. There is a person called "the Son" or "Jesus" who is also called "God." The apostle Thomas, after seeing the resurrected Jesus, said to him, "My Lord and my God!" (John 20:28).

And the Holy Spirit. There is also a person called "the Holy Spirit" who is also equated with God. In Acts 5:3–4 the apostle Peter rebukes a man named Ananias, saying that he has lied to the Holy Spirit. Peter then continues his rebuke: "You have not lied to men, but to God." Lying to the Holy Spirit then is the same as lying to God.

Three Distinct Persons

The Father, the Son, and the Holy Spirit are three distinct persons—personal beings who possess will, intelligence, and emotion—who exist at the same time. This means that the Father is not the Son, the Father is not the Holy Spirit, and the Son is not the Holy Spirit. We must never confuse the three persons. Each one has an identity, though the three are in complete and perfect unity as the one God.

We see in the Bible the distinction of the persons of the Trinity in many ways. For example, the Son prays to the Father (Matthew 26:39). At Jesus' baptism the Father and the Holy Spirit are present. The Spirit of God descends like a dove, and the Father says, "This is My beloved Son, in whom I am well-pleased" (Matthew 3:17). In these examples the persons of the

Trinity are present at the same time. In the New Testament we also find that the Father sends the Son: "In this is love, not that we loved God, but that He loved us and sent His Son to be the propitiation for our sins" (1 John 4:10). The fact that the Father sends the Son implies two persons, as the sending of the Holy Spirit implies a third (John 14:26).

For Discussion

1. What three essential statements comprise the Trinity doctrine?
2. What do each of the three statements teach?
3. Why are the three statements important in our understanding of the Trinity doctrine?

Beyond the Basics

The first four centuries of the Christian Church featured many discussions and debates concerning the nature of God. Questions arose as to how one could affirm the biblical witness of one God and still remain true to the biblical witness that the Father, the Son, and the Holy Spirit were in Scripture each called God.

During these years answers to these questions were given, but some were not orthodox. Indeed they were quite heretical. The early Church rose to the occasion to pronounce what was true in the Scriptures, but this did not stop the spread of error altogether. And to this day we see the very same errors propagated by many cults. Because of the dilemma of how "one" can be "three," statements arise to solve it, but, again, these statements are far removed from Christian orthodoxy.

Some groups espouse that Jesus and the Holy Spirit are not God at all. Here a neat but erroneous package is given: Jesus is the Son of God, they say, but not God himself. Likewise the Spirit is not God but is rather the "force" God uses to accomplish the divine will. Others maintain that there is one God but attempt to resolve the three-in-one dilemma by saying that there is only one person in the **Godhead:** the Son, who can switch "modes" and become the Father at certain times and the Holy Spirit at other times. This is known as **modalism.**

Christians have wrestled with understanding the Trinity for centuries. In that undertaking, some popular analogies have emerged. No doubt, you yourself have encountered them. I will examine three of these near the end of this chapter.

A Contradiction?

Is there a contradiction in the phrase "God is one and three"? Yes. But the Bible does not teach simply that God is one and three. Further, "one God, three Gods" is also a contradiction— an ancient heresy known as **tritheism.** The Bible does not teach that either. The Bible describes one God, three persons. Do you see the difference? Simply stating "God is one and three" falls short. We must ask, "One *what,* and three *what?*" If the answers to "what" are two *different* things, no contradiction arises. Thus, there is no contradiction in saying that God is one God in three *persons.*

Some Presuppositions

A *presupposition* is a fact already accepted as true before a discussion begins. There are three presuppositions that I will state before examining the doctrine of the Trinity. Each of these presuppositions can be defended, but the defense of them does not fall within the scope of this book (see the suggested readings on p. 101 for good books on the subject). The three are

1. The Bible is the Word of God.

2. We are finite in understanding.

3. God is infinite in understanding.

Given these presuppositions, we conclude, then, that we do not fully know *how* the one God is the Father and the Son and the Holy Spirit. We just do not know the "hows" of it all. But we do fully know *that* the one God is the Father and the Son and the Holy Spirit because it is revealed in the Bible.

The Father

Because God's self-revelation came to a patriarchal and tribal culture, God was revealed as "Father" (see chap. 2 for study of the Son and chap. 3 for the Holy Spirit). In this way God's people would better understand their relationship to God.

God as Father in the Old Testament. God states of the nation of Israel, "Israel is My Son, My first-born" (Exodus 4:22), meaning that Israel is preeminent over all the nations and will inherit the Father's kingdom. God's people state, "Now, O LORD, Thou art our Father" (Isaiah 64:8). Here God is Father because God's people have a relationship with the LORD by faith. In the New Testament we are told specifically that those who have faith in Jesus are the Father's children by adoption (Romans 8:15–16; see chap. 7 under "Adoption").

Additionally, God is the "Father" because from all eternity and forever God has a relationship with his Son, Jesus Christ (John 1:18). In this relationship, which uniquely and eternally belongs to Jesus because of who he is (our relationship with the Father is by adoption; not so with Jesus), Jesus prayed to and named God as Father (John 17:1).

God as Father in the New Testament. "God" is the most frequent designation of the Father in the New Testament. When the designation "God the Father" occurs, there is little doubt, but when "God" is used alone, it most often (though not always) means "the Father." Without this understanding, one is likely to be confused as to which person of the Trinity the writers of Scripture are referring to when they use the word.

For example, to which person of the Trinity does "God" refer in 1 Peter 2:19: "For this finds favor, if for the sake of conscience toward God a man bears up under sorrows when suffering unjustly"? Simply go to the beginning of Peter's letter. Here we read in 1:2 that Christians are chosen "according to the foreknowledge of God the Father." As the verse continues, Peter makes a distinction between God the Father and the other two persons of the Trinity, adding "by the sanctifying work of the Spirit, that you may obey Jesus Christ." So the answer is that "God" in 2 Peter 2:19 refers to the Father. (This is not to say that Peter does not view Jesus as God, for in 2 Peter 1:1 he calls Jesus "our God and Savior.")

Another example occurs when James writes, "God cannot be

tempted" (1:13). Here as well he refers to the Father. Note the beginning of his epistle: "James, a bond-servant of God and of the Lord Jesus Christ" (1:1). Note as well the distinction of the persons of the Father and Jesus.*

To sum up, remember that "God" most often refers to the Father, though that this is not always the case. When trying to decide whether or not "God" means "the Father," skim the book or epistle and look for the distinctions I mentioned above.

Distinguishing between Father, Son, and Holy Spirit

There is no direct statement in the Bible such as "God is the Father and the Son and the Holy Spirit." (If anyone asks *why* this is so, remember that this question erroneously implies that the Bible must phrase it the way we want it in our culture and in our way of putting it! The doctrine of the Trinity as we know it was not fully articulated itself by the early Church until the fourth century.) But there are statements that were quite direct to first-century readers. Some of these relate to what the three persons of the Trinity do, while at least one relates to their very nature or being.

---

*Some people use this verse to deny that Jesus is God. They say, "Jesus was tempted by Satan, yet here it says that God cannot be tempted. How, then, can you say Jesus is God?" When we understand that in James 1:13 "God" refers to the Father, the problem is solved!

One verse in particular is used to deny that Jesus is God. The argument goes something like this: "People saw Jesus when he was on the earth. But the Bible states that no one has seen God at any time. Jesus, then, cannot be God!" The verse referred to is John 1:18. Here we read, "No man has seen God at any time; the only begotten God, who is in the bosom of the Father, He has explained Him." Often John uses the word "God" to refer to the Father (not always; see John 20:28). Key here is John 6:46 because it shows us that "God" means "Father" and specifically identifies who it is that no one has seen: "Not that any man has seen the Father, except the one who is from God; He has seen the Father." So John 1:18 teaches that no one has seen the Father and that the only begotten God (Jesus) has explained him (that is, the Father). In this verse the first use of "God" is for the Father, the second use of "God" is for the Son.

Theology based on function. Most verses teaching the doctrine of the Trinity occur in the context of what God—as Father, Son, and Holy Spirit—*does*. These are called "functional (or economic) trinitarian verses." Following are some examples. Before we start, however, note that despite the Father's and the Son's and the Holy Spirit's performance of distinct acts, no person of the Trinity ever acts outside the sphere of the other two persons. Stating this another way, even though the acts of each person are distinct, each one acts in unity with the other two persons of the Trinity.

To bring about the salvation of the Christian, the triune God has acted. We read in 1 Peter 1:1–2 that Christians are "chosen according to the foreknowledge of God the Father, by the sanctifying work of the Spirit, that you may obey Jesus Christ and be sprinkled with His blood." The process of our salvation began when from all eternity God the Father chose us according to his foreknowledge. We are also *sanctified* by the Holy Spirit, that is, made holy and set apart for service to God, which is, of course, a very important part of our lives as Christians. Then the goal is stated: that we may obey Jesus Christ and enjoy the fullness of his salvation. Quite clearly Peter is reminding his readers of their faith in the triune God with words that inform of what the Deity has done for them.

The apostle Paul mentions aspects of the ministries of the three persons of the Trinity in closing his second letter to the Christians at Corinth: "The grace of the Lord Jesus Christ, and the love of God [the Father; see the first three verses of chap. 1], and the fellowship of the Holy Spirit, be with you all." Here the triune God's grace, love, and fellowship are Paul's appeal to the church. Because Christians are indeed blessed with grace, love, and fellowship, they are to experience them in their daily walk with God. This experience only comes because it is the Son who grants grace, the Father who expresses love, and the Spirit who is present with (and in) the people of the triune God. All three persons act for the well-being of the people of God.

Theology based on being. In addition to biblical passages that teach us what the triune God *does*, which is known as the "functional (or economic) Trinity," at least one verse teaches us what God *is*, which is known as the "ontological (or essential) Trinity." The word "ontological" comes from the two Greek words *ontōs* (being, essence, really) and *logos* (discourse) and thus means "a statement having to do with the being or essence of something."

The following passage teaches us what God *is* (though, as we shall see, it is not completely devoid of teaching us what God *does*). The Great Commission of Matthew 28:19–20 is Christ's command to his disciples to "make disciples of all the nations, baptizing them in the name of the Father and the Son and the Holy Spirit, teaching them to observe all that I commanded you." In other words, Christians are to preach the gospel and make "learners" of all nations. Then, what characterizes Christians is that they are baptized, signifying that they have come into **covenant** relationship with the one God or "name" (the Father and the Son and the Holy Spirit), and that they are taught to obey Christ.

What concerns us is the phrase "the name of the Father and the Son and the Holy Spirit." First, notice that "name" is in the singular; there are not three names, but one. Second, note that the one name is "the Father and the Son and the Holy Spirit." What can we learn from this statement? The very way it is constructed tells us a great deal. According to a basic rule of Greek grammar, two or more personal and singular nouns (not proper names, such as John, Luke, Matthew) separated by "and" (Greek *kai*) and each preceded by the definite article ("the") are understood to be distinct nouns. Since "the Father and the Son and the Holy Spirit" contains two or more separate, singular personal nouns separated by "and" and each preceded by the definite article, we should understand them as three distinct persons.

Let's look again at Matthew 28:19. The one "name" is "the Father and the Son and the Holy Spirit." This is why Christians believe that the one God is the Father and the Son and the Holy Spirit. This is why Christians believe that three distinct persons are the one God.

Greek grammar rule

Using Analogies

When it comes to explaining or understanding the doctrine of the Trinity, I do not like using analogies. In other areas of study, analogies are helpful, but in the case of the Trinity they suggest some form of error.

Take, for example, the "water exists as steam, liquid, and ice" analogy. Though it is true that water can exist in three different forms, one body of water does not exist as steam, liquid, and ice *simultaneously*. With the Trinity, the three persons exist *at the same time; otherwise, we fall into modalism* (the view that one person switches between modes of existence: Father at one time, then Son, then Holy Spirit).

Another popular analogy was once suggested to me as a "quick and to the point" way of understanding the Trinity. At a local church, after I spent a fair amount of time expounding on the doctrine from Scripture, a woman explained that she understood the Trinity by analogy with her own life: "I am a wife, a mother, and a businesswoman." I pointed out that this too suggests modalism—one person, three modes.

Finally, some analogies indicate that God is made up of "parts"—as in one pie, three slices. Also popular is the egg analogy: one egg has shell, white, and yolk. These as well suggest error, for God is not made up of parts. Colossians 2:9 states that in Christ "all the fulness of Deity dwells in bodily form." Is Christ, then, a *part* of God? No, and when we take our cue from Colossians 2:9, we may also presume that the Father and the Spirit each possess deity completely and fully.

Never Say "Never"

Since God is infinite, the Trinity is ultimately incomprehensible. That is to say, it follows that we will reach a point at which we have to admit that we can go no further. But the key here is "reach a point."

Many non-Christians have shared with me that when they went to Christians to get an explanation of the doctrine of the Trinity, they were told at the start, "We can never understand that!" May that never be true of us. The right thing to do is show people from Scripture *what* we believe and *why* we believe it. Of course, there will be a time when we say, "I can go no further," but the goal is striving until we reach that point.

For Discussion

1. The Bible is the Word of God and describes for us one God, three persons. It does not fully answer the question of *how* this is so. Why is this enough for Christians to know?

2. Why is there no contradiction in the phrase "one God, three persons"?

3. "God" is often (not always) a synonym for the Father. Ask a person in your discussion group to explain a biblical passage in which this is so.

4. The biblical writers convey the Trinity in the functional sense, that is, by what God *does*. The Trinity doctrine, therefore, is not an abstract principle. In what sense does the Trinity doctrine have meaning for all believers?

5. The biblical writers also convey the Trinity in the ontological sense, that is, by what God *is*. How does an ontological statement of the Trinity differ from a functional statement of the Trinity? In what way(s) do they complement each other? In other words, how does the functional imply the ontological, and vice versa?

6. Why should you stay away from analogies when teaching others the doctrine of the Trinity? If you desire to use an analogy, how would you guard against the errors documented in this chapter? What other errors can arise from analogies?

7. When teaching others the doctrine of the Trinity, we sometimes arrive at the point when we say, "This is as far as I can go; we can never fully comprehend this doctrine." Why is it important to stop at this certain point?

8. Why must we never say at the outset that we cannot understand the doctrine of the Trinity?

✚ Meditations

Our Triune God Owns Us

"Go therefore and make disciples of all the nations, baptizing them in the name of the Father and the Son and the Holy Spirit." (Matthew 28:19)

One characteristic of being a disciple—of being saved—is baptism. When we are baptized, these words are most likely spoken: "I baptize you in the name of the Father and the Son and the Holy Spirit." There is significant meaning behind these words.

When a covenant is made, you can expect to find that God claims to "own" his people. God said to them through Isaiah: "I have called you by name; / you are Mine!" When Jesus commands his disciples to baptize in the name of the triune God, he is saying that disciples come under the ownership, the authority, of the triune God. Think for a moment. Could there be anything better than to be owned by God? Could anything compare to the God of the universe saying, "You are Mine!"?

Everyone in the world has an owner, and owners usually command those whom they own. These owners become the lords of our lives. Owners range from inanimate things to people. Possessions can own us, and so can other people, including us thinking we own ourselves. But all these fall short. All these will fail us.

If you answered the above questions, saying, "No, nothing compares to God's owning me," it is cause for rejoicing. The triune God owns you through the joys of life as well as through the trials and persecutions and tragedies of our existence. This is what it means to be a disciple.

Great triune God, thank you for making me your own. Help me to trust you with all my heart and with all of my life. In Christ, amen.

Our Triune God Acts

Chosen according to the foreknowledge of God the Father, by the sanctifying work of the Spirit, that you may obey Jesus Christ and be sprinkled with His blood. (1 Peter 1:1–2)

Part of knowing who God *is* involves knowing what God *does*. Knowing what the Deity has done for us grounds our worship of

God. Christians are chosen by the Father and enjoy the sanctifying work of the Holy Spirit for the purpose of obedience to Christ.

Before all things came into being by the command of the eternal triune God, God chose us to be his own! God purposed to have an intimate relationship with us. That happened a very long time ago. What does that say to us now? Right now the Holy Spirit is sanctifying us, bringing us more and more into conformity with the will of the Father for our lives. All this, says Peter, comes about for the express purpose of obedience to our Lord Jesus Christ.

When I think of these acts of the triune God, when I contemplate them (really contemplate them) in my heart, a paradox arises. When I consider God—when I in my finitude consider who the Deity is—I know how insignificant I am! And yet I am significant because *in God* I enjoy the worth of being God's own child.

In view of God's acts for us, can we not help but run to the throne of grace? And then when we are on our knees at that throne worshiping God, wonder of wonders, the Holy Spirit gently reminds us that God is the reason we are here in worship in the first place!

2
God the Son

THE APOSTLE PAUL POSSESSED SOME IMPRESSIVE CREDENTIALS! He was a Hebrew of Hebrews, circumcised the eighth day, from the tribe of Benjamin, a Pharisee, educated under Gamaliel, and as to the law found blameless (Philippians 3:5–6; Acts 22:3). If anyone could boast, it was Paul.

Yet Paul said, "I count all things to be loss in view of the surpassing value of knowing Christ Jesus my Lord" (Philippians 3:8). Knowing Christ, having an intimate relationship with Christ, was of paramount importance for this exemplar of the faith. Implied in this verse as well is the importance of knowing *who* Christ is. After all, to know someone is to know about that person, and the qualities of that person are vital to the act of knowing him. Are they not?

Knowing the Son of God (and knowing about him) is the bedrock of Christianity. Christianity stands or falls on the person of Christ. The **doctrine** therefore warrants our deepest attention.

The Basics

Jesus is the Son of God (and God the Son), the second **person** of the Trinity. He always, from all eternity, existed as the Son of God. In order to walk among us, Jesus joined to his full deity a full human nature so that from his conception as the one and

15

only God-man he eternally remains both God and man. In this section we shall explore both the deity of Christ and the humanity of Christ.

The Deity of Christ

The Bible declares that Jesus is God. Following is a sampling of the many passages that affirm the deity of Christ.

John 1:1. The last part of this verse reads, "The Word was God." To whom does John refer when he writes "the Word"? Verse 14 gives us a strong clue: "The Word became flesh, and dwelt among us." John is not talking about the Bible when he mentions "the Word." Rather, in John 1:1 he is teaching us about the **preincarnate** Jesus. So before Jesus "became flesh" (John 1:14), he was God.

Well, was Jesus always God? Certainly, for if God is by definition eternal, then Jesus was always God. Therefore, there never was a time when Jesus *became* God. Our next verse will further aid us in understanding that Jesus existed as God the Son before his **incarnation.**

John 8:58. Here Jesus says, "Before Abraham was born, I am." What was Jesus claiming? He was claiming to be what God claims to be.

In Exodus 3:14 we read that "God said to Moses, 'I AM WHO I AM'; and He said, 'Thus you shall say to the sons of Israel, "I AM has sent me to you."'" God's self-identification is "I AM." Jesus' is the same, and moreover he claims to have been I AM even before Abraham came into existence. This is why **Christians** believe in Jesus' preincarnate deity.

The Son who is sent. Yet another fact shows that Jesus preexisted (see **preexistence**). It is the fact that Jesus was *sent* by the Father.

God the Father sent his Son into the world. This theme occurs frequently throughout the New Testament (Mark 9:37, for example), but what does it mean? By way of analogy, think of what is signified when you send a friend to the grocery store. Your action signifies that you were with your friend prior to when she arrived at the store and was seen by others. In like manner Jesus had to have existed with his Father prior to the Father's sending him into the world. Also considering other verses that tell of Christ's deity, we then conclude that Jesus pre-existed as God the Son.

Matthew 1:23. The Bible also teaches Jesus' incarnate deity: "'BEHOLD, THE VIRGIN SHALL BE WITH CHILD, AND SHALL BEAR A SON, AND THEY SHALL CALL HIS NAME IMMANUEL,' which translated means, 'GOD WITH US.'" With the birth of Jesus, we have "God with us." This is much more than God's being with us *through* Jesus (as if Jesus were someone that merely represented God). In Jesus we have God among us (see also John 1:14). Matthew 1:23 is a quotation from Isaiah 7:14. Later the prophet Isaiah was to call this Son the "Mighty God" (Isaiah 9:6).

John 20:28. This scene describes one of the postresurrection appearances of the Lord Jesus. Thomas doubts that the other apostles had seen the Lord after his resurrection. Eight days later the apostles are gathered again, this time with Thomas. Jesus appears. Thomas then "said to Him, 'My Lord and my God!'" This is quite a confession for a **monotheist** to make! Thomas, of course, believed that the Father was his God. Here he states that Jesus is his God. All Christians are to make the same confession.

The Humanity of Christ

Unlike his deity, Jesus' humanity had a beginning in time. John writes that Jesus' flesh "became" (John 1:14). Paul teaches that "He . . . was revealed in the flesh" (1 Timothy 3:16). Even now, in his resurrected and exalted state as God the Son, he is called "the man Christ Jesus" (1 Timothy 2:5).

Other things about Jesus cue us to the fact that he was human. Jesus was conceived and developed in the womb of his mother (Matthew 1:21–23; Luke 1:35). He was born, as are all humans (Galatians 4:4). Jesus grew up (Luke 2:42). He thirsted (John 19:28), hungered (Matthew 4:2), grew tired (John 4:6), and experienced human emotions (John 11:35). And we must not forget that Jesus died (John 19:33).

Fully God and Fully Man

The Christian's confession, then, is that Jesus is both God and man. Further, Christians believe that Jesus is *fully* God (Colossians 2:9) and *fully* human (Hebrews 2:17). In Colossians 2:9 Paul writes that in Jesus "all the fulness of Deity dwells in bodily form." Hebrews 2:17 conveys that Jesus was "made like His brethren in all things" (or "in every respect"). That is to say, Jesus shared truly and fully in our makeup as human beings, the exception being that he was without sin (Hebrews 4:15).

Jesus as Unique

Jesus is the *only* one who was, is, and ever will be both God and man. In other words, Jesus is unique. This is what the apostle John means when he calls Jesus the "only begotten" (John 1:14). He is the Father's unique Son. Further, because Jesus is the *only* begotten, he alone is the way of salvation for all humanity. In John 14:6 Jesus claims, "I am the way, and the truth, and the life; no one comes to the Father, but through Me."

For Discussion

1. Jesus is the Son of God (and God the Son). Can you think of one or two Bible verses to support this?

2. Did Jesus exist before his incarnation? Did Jesus exist as God, the second person of the Trinity, before his incarnation?

3. Is Jesus both fully God and fully man? Give a Scripture verse for each.

Beyond the Basics

The Importance of Christology

 Christianity stands or falls with **Christology.** Why? In one very important sense, Christianity is a relationship. To be a Christian means to be in a relationship with Jesus Christ (and, as a result, with the Father and the Holy Spirit). Defining the relationship is vital and in part can be discussed within the framework of salvation and its natural outgrowth, obedience or sanctification (see chap. 8). But defining the person with whom Christians are in relationship is classified as Christology. But why is defining that person so important? The answer comes from Jesus himself in John 8:24.

Some background is necessary for understanding the implications of John 8:24. In John 8:58 Jesus says, "Before Abraham was born, I am (Greek *egō eimi*)." "I am" comes from Exodus 3:14 (where an equivalent Greek phrase is used in the **LXX:** *ho ōn*, "the One who is" or "the Being") and is a title used by God. Jesus' claim, therefore, had tremendous implications—he claimed to be God.

The Jews knew of Jesus' claim, which in their eyes was in violation of Leviticus 24:16: "The alien [foreigner] as well as the native [Israelite], when he blasphemes the Name [of God], shall be put to death." This is why one verse after Jesus' claim in John 8:58 they pick up rocks to stone Jesus to death. The Jews knew the implications of such a claim by Jesus. Let's look at some of them.

"I AM" in the Old Testament comes from the Hebrew *ani hu*, which literally means "I am he." This saying of the historical Jesus in John 8:58 is based upon that Hebrew term, specifically upon the LXX (or **Septuagint**). In Deuteronomy 32:39, for example, God says, "See now that I, I am He." The LXX here reads "I AM" *(egō eimi)* for the Hebrew *ani hu*. The point is that Jesus claims for himself in John 8:58 the divine name of God cited in the LXX.

In John 8:24 Jesus is dialoguing with the religious leaders and says to them, "Unless you believe that I AM *(egō eimi)*, you shall die in your sins" (my translation). Some translations have "I am *He*," with "He" in italics because it is not in the original Greek, though it rightly conveys the Hebrew *ani hu*. The *New International Version* (NIV) has "I am" followed by "the one I claim to be" in brackets, again because this phrase is not in the original.

The point is that anyone who intently denies who Christ claims to be—specifically I AM—will die in their sins. Jesus' words provide a sober warning to those who would deny who he is. His words are also a sober reminder to Christians that Christology is important—so important that one's eternal destiny rests upon what one thinks of Christ.

The Deity of Christ

There are scores of verses that teach the deity of Christ. Let's selectively look at two in some detail.

John 1:1. This three-part verse is packed with themes relating the deity of Jesus: "In the beginning was the Word, and the Word was with God, and the Word was God."

Jesus' *eternal existence* is taught in the first part: "In the beginning was the Word." With the phrase "In the beginning," John wants us to go back to the very beginning of all things! Genesis 1:1 reads, "In the beginning God created the heavens and the earth." In effect, John is saying to his readers, "When everything that was created *was* created, the Word [Greek *logos;* the preincarnate Christ] already 'was.'" Significant here is that little word "was"(Greek *ēn*). It means so very much, for it signifies "existing continuously"! Thus John communicates to us that even before the creation of all things, Jesus (as the Word) already was there! He existed eternally!

Jesus' *eternal existence with the Father* is taught in the second part: "the Word was with God." The word "was" once again signifies "existing continuously." So the Word eternally was with the Father. Is it reasonable to think that "God" refers to the Father? I believe it does, for two reasons. First, God is often a synonym for the Father (as discussed in chap. 1). Second, 1 John 1:2 (John's first epistle, not the Gospel of John) mentions "the eternal life [Jesus], which was with the Father and was manifested to us." Notice that John specifically mentions that Jesus was with the Father. There is no reason not to assume the same in John 1:1.

Jesus' *eternal nature as God* is taught in the third and final part of John 1:1: "The Word was God." "God" in this part of the verse functions differently from "God" in the second part, which is translated as "the Word was with God." (The difference in function is conveyed in the Greek both by word order and the case of the noun.) Though in the second part "God" refers to the Father, here in the third part it refers to *Jesus' essential nature.* In other words, the Word is by nature God. He is by nature deity in the fullest sense. Stated in another way, what the Father is by nature, the Son is as well.

The teaching of John in the second and third parts of John 1:1 shows the relationship of the Father to the Son within the doctrine of the Trinity. The distinction of the persons of the Father and the Son is seen in the second part of John 1:1 ("the Word was with God"—the Word was *with* the Father). And the oneness of the divine nature (one God) is maintained in the third part ("the Word was God"); that is, the Word is of the same nature as the Father.

John 20:28. This is perhaps the most direct statement found in the Bible to show that Jesus is God: "Thomas answered and said to Him, 'My Lord and my God!'"

The Greek for "my Lord and my God" is *ho kurios mou kai ho theos mou,* which is stiffly translated "the Lord of me and the God of me." Rather than an exclamation of Thomas's surprise, this is a quotation from the LXX of Psalm 35:23. In the psalm the writer addresses God and cries, "Stir up Thyself, and awake to my right, / And to my cause, my God and my Lord *(ho theos mou kai ho kurios mou)."* Thomas says, "My Lord and my God"; the psalmist writes, "My God and my Lord." Though the order is reversed, Thomas's words come directly from the LXX. The apostle confesses Jesus as his God.

Ontological and Functional Christology

In chapter 1 the terms "ontological" and "functional" were defined in the context of the Trinity. Christology as well utilizes these terms. Ontological (from the Greek word *ontōs* for "being") Christology is concerned with what Christ *is,* while functional Christology deals with what Christ *does.*

The last part of John 1:1 ("the Word was God") is primarily an ontological statement—it says something about the nature of Christ; that is, he is by nature God. Scripture, however, contains far more references to what Christ does. Yet a very interesting truth arises from the study of functional christological passages: the functional implies the ontological. By this I mean that what Jesus does (functional) implies what Jesus is by nature (ontological). Before we look at some examples of this, it is necessary to make the connection between what Jesus does in the New Testament and what God does in the Old Testament.

Yahweh. The Hebrew word *Yahweh* is one of the names of the true and living God. Since it is a Hebrew word, we find it in the Old Testament. In many translations of the Old Testament you will come across "LORD." Notice that all the letters are capitalized. Whenever you see "LORD," the Hebrew is *Yahweh.*

The following three New Testament passages depict Jesus as doing things (past, present, and future) that only Yahweh does, thus showing that Jesus is Yahweh the Son. (A "reference edition" of the Bible will assist you in finding many more such verses. I recommend the reference edition of the New American Standard Bible.)

Mark 2:5. Jesus says, "My son, your sins are forgiven." Jesus forgives sin. The scribes who heard Jesus' utterance said, "Who can forgive sins but God alone?" (v. 7). They were right! Only God can forgive sin.

In Isaiah 43:25 Yahweh states, "I, even I, am the one who wipes out your transgressions for My own sake; / And I will not remember your sins." We know that it is Yahweh (the LORD) who speaks because of the declaration in verse 14: "Thus says the LORD your Redeemer." Thus, by his actions Jesus is claiming to do that which Yahweh does. And the functional implies the ontological—Jesus is therefore Yahweh the Son.

Matthew 8:26. The second part of this verse reads, "Then He arose, and rebuked the winds and the sea; and it became perfectly calm." When Jesus stills the storm, what is he saying about himself?

Jesus is saying that he is Yahweh the Son. Psalm 107:29 reads, "He caused the storm to be still, / So that the waves of the sea were hushed." Who does this? Yahweh does (see "LORD" in vv. 1–2,6,8,13, etc.).

Matthew 24:30. The last half of this verse states, "They will see the SON OF MAN COMING ON THE CLOUDS OF THE SKY with power and great glory." In Isaiah 19:1 Yahweh is the cloud-rider, and his coming on the clouds is associated with judgment. Judgment is also associated with Jesus' coming on the clouds (Matthew 24:31). Again, what Jesus does implies who he is—Yahweh the Son.

Son of God Means God the Son

Transposing the two nouns in the phrase "Son of God" doesn't alter the meaning. That is, "Son of God" and "God the Son" mean the same thing. Some people attempt to deny the deity of Christ by stating, "He's not God; he's the *Son* of God." But ironically, "Son of God" means "God the Son." Two reasons for this follow.

First, the Jews tried to stone Jesus for his claim that he is the Son of God (John 19:7). Now the Jews knew that others were called "sons of God" (Genesis 6:2; Luke 3:38), so they would not have wanted to stone Jesus for being in *that* category. They would want to stone him, however, if by the phrase "Son of God" he was saying something about who he was (ontologically). This is why the Jews said, "We have a law, and by that law He ought to die because He made Himself out to be the Son of God" (John 19:7). What was that law? Leviticus 24:16. Jesus was blaspheming the Name (claiming to be God).

Second, in John 5:18 the Jews sought to kill Jesus because he "was calling God His own Father, making Himself equal with God." In calling God his own Father, Jesus was claiming to be the Son of God. And by claiming that, Jesus was making himself *equal* with God the Father on ontological grounds. In this verse "equal" means "equal in nature and authority." Thus, in John 5:18 "Son of God" is an ontological claim—it means "God the Son."

Only Begotten

John 1:14 teaches that Jesus is *monogenēs* (only begotten) from the Father. This word, which means "unique," comes from two Greek words: *monos* (alone, one) and *genos* (kind). Jesus, then, is "one of a kind," thus unique.

Additionally, the context tells us that "unique" is the meaning. Notice that John never calls Christians "sons" of God. He always refers to us as "children." "Son" is a loaded term for John, and he reserves it only for Jesus. In fact, just two verses before John calls Jesus "the only begotten," he calls believers "children of God" (John 1:12). Thus John distinguishes between Jesus as *the* Son of God and us as "children of God."

The Two Natures and One Person of Christ

Christ is fully God and fully human, which means he is deity in the truest and fullest sense and human in the truest and fullest sense. Yet Christian **orthodoxy** maintains that Jesus Christ is one person and that the one person Jesus Christ has two natures (divine and human). Christ possesses these two natures in all their fullness, without mixture or separation. The two natures do not mix, for if they did, Jesus would be neither really human nor really deity. And at the same time the two natures cannot be separated. That is, whenever Jesus says or does something, the whole person of Christ says it or does it. In other words, the two natures are *united* in the one person of Jesus of Nazareth.

Consider the life of Jesus: when Jesus hungers, when he thirsts, when he says, "I AM," and when he graciously dies on the cross. In these events, how do we formulate the relationship of the two natures in the one person? I suggest this formula: *By virtue of Christ's* _____ *nature, the one (whole, complete) person of Christ could* _____. We now fill in the blanks: By virtue of his human nature, the one person of Christ hungered. By virtue of his divine nature, the one person of Christ could say, "I AM."

For Discussion

1. Why is Christology so important?

2. Is Jesus portrayed in ontological and functional categories?

3. How does the functional imply the ontological?

4. Why does "Son of God" mean "God the Son"?

5. In the one person of Christ are two natures, divine and human, each possessed in their fullness. The two natures are united in Christ without mixture or separation. What dangers are there in mixing or separating the two natures?

6. Discuss the negative implications of mixing or separating Christ's two natures as they pertain to his work on the cross (see Hebrews 2:14–17).

✛ Meditations

Count All Things as Loss

More than that, I count all things to be loss in view of the surpassing value of knowing Christ Jesus my Lord, for whom I have suffered the loss of all things, and count them but rubbish in order that I may gain Christ. (Philippians 3:8)

Nothing in this world can compare to knowing the Lord Jesus Christ. Take a moment to think about what that means. Yes, I know how high an example the apostle Paul has set for us. He was a man of faith. Anything he could have put confidence in (Philippians 3:4–6) was but rubbish compared to knowing Jesus, and for good reason, for what can compare to being resurrected and being with the Lord forever (vv. 11,21)? For Paul there was no contest.

Imagine! Imagine one day being in the presence of the God of the universe, glorifying and enjoying the Deity forever. Imagine one day doing this with your family and friends who knew the Lord. Can anything in this world compare?

When we desire to "know" someone, we invest in that someone and make every effort to find out about him or her. And the key here is desire; isn't it? In that someone is something that attracts us, that causes in us the desire to know that someone. Then when we really know someone, we begin to act like that person. Have you ever noticed this phenomenon?

For Christians, all that Jesus is (fully God and fully human) and all that he has done for us and our salvation should be the attraction. In view of who Christ is and what he has done for us, it can be no other way. Thus Paul desired to know Christ. And for Paul, there was no one else that he wanted to be like. Can we say the same?

Who else but you, Lord Jesus, should receive my utmost desire to know. I echo the words of the apostle Paul: "I count all things to be loss in view of the surpassing value of knowing Christ Jesus my Lord." Today I make a commitment to seek you, to learn about you, to know you. Give me the strength and the desire to do so. In this year to come, please reveal yourself to me so that I might come to know you better. Amen.

Jesus Becomes One of Us

And the Word became flesh. (John 1:14)

Here John focuses not so much on the virgin birth as on the fact that God the Son has come to dwell with his people. The eternal Word who is God the Son (John 1:1) now comes and takes on full humanity. Jesus is not only fully God; he as well becomes fully human.

Jesus' flesh "became." That is to say, the eternal God the Son, in an act of immeasurable, infinite love, now unites with his eternal deity full humanity. He as the Word always "was." His flesh, his full human nature, however, came into existence. Jesus now experiences something that he never had before all ages past—humanity.

By virtue of his taking on a full human nature, Jesus can be tangibly seen. Even though no human has seen God the Father at any time, Jesus' full humanity becomes the vehicle by which he could reveal the Father to us (see John 1:18; compare 6:46).

"The Word became flesh." God has become one of us! Why? To redeem us, to live a righteous and perfect life on our behalf, and to present that perfect and righteous life to the Father, culminating with his death on the cross in our place. This is the love of the Father, that God the Son would come, experience everything we as humans experience (except sin in all its manifestations), die on the cross, and take away from us the Father's wrath. Such grace.

Our precious Savior, the Lord Jesus Christ, has taken on our humanity. God, yes, God, has done this. The holy Son of God has given himself for us. For us! I cannot fully comprehend such mercy. I cannot. But I can, and do, fall on my knees in humble, sorrowful, yet joyful adoration of him who is to be praised forever. Jesus, we praise you.

3

God the Holy Spirit

IN YOUR **CHRISTIAN** WALK, NEVER FORGET THIS: WHEN WE become followers of Christ, we are to have an intimate relationship with the Holy Spirit. And never forget this as well: In that intimate relationship we should desire to know him better.

The basic Christian confession of the Holy Spirit, the third **person** of the Trinity, is that the Spirit is God and is a person. Moreover, the Spirit is the person of the Trinity who sets the Christian apart for service to God and is the giver of gifts that enable the Christian to perform that service.

The Basics

The Holy Spirit Is a Person

The Spirit is a person with will, intellect, and emotion. Paul states that the Holy Spirit distributes divine gifts "just as He wills" (1 Corinthians 12:11; see the list of these gifts in vv. 8–10). That the Spirit has intellect is seen in 1 Corinthians 2:11: "Even so the thoughts of God no one knows except the Spirit of God." Only someone with intellectual capacity knows the thoughts of someone. And the Spirit possesses the emotion of grief. Paul exhorts the Christians at Ephesus with these words: "Do not grieve the Holy Spirit of God" (Ephesians 4:30).

The Holy Spirit Is God

Although the evidence for the deity of the Holy Spirit is not as abundant as the evidence for the deity of the Father and the Son, there is clear teaching in the Bible that the Spirit is God.

In Acts 5:3–4 Peter rebukes Ananias. Ananias and his wife, Sapphira, had sold a piece of property (v. 1) but had kept back some of the money for themselves (v. 2). Verses 3 and 4 read: "But Peter said, 'Ananias, why has Satan filled your heart to lie to the Holy Spirit, and to keep back some of the price of the land? . . . You have not lied to men, but to God.'" Here Peter equates lying to the Holy Spirit with lying to God. To lie to the Spirit *is* to lie to God.

Our Relationship with the Spirit

Because the Holy Spirit is a person and not some ambiguous "force," we as persons can have a relationship with the Spirit. Because the Spirit is God, we therefore have a relationship with God. This most exciting aspect of the Christian walk is one that has been greatly neglected by many Christians.

Get to know the Holy Spirit more intimately. Pray to the Spirit, asking for whatever gifts the Spirit wants you to have for Christian service. There are many gifts of the Spirit. Romans 12:6–8 lists prophecy, service, teaching, exhortation, giving, leading, and mercy. Listed in 1 Corinthians 12:8–11 are the gifts of wisdom, knowledge, faith, healing, miracles, prophecy, ability to discern spirits, tongues, and interpretation of tongues. Ephesians 4:11 includes apostles, prophets, evangelists, pastors, and teachers. Finally, 1 Peter 4:11 lists speaking the utterances of God and service. Study the Scriptures in order to know the Spirit better.

For Discussion

1. Why do we confess the Holy Spirit as God? Can you give some Bible verses to support this?

2. Is the Holy Spirit a person? Can you give some Bible verses to support this as well?

3. Why can we have a personal relationship with the Holy Spirit?

4. How is this personal relationship with the Holy Spirit culti-
vated and reinforced in our lives?

Beyond the Basics

Pneumatology, the study of the Holy Spirit, starts with two
basic categories—personhood and deity. We will start with more
evidence for the personality of the Spirit, then move to more evidence of his deity, followed by a study of the work of the Spirit.

The Personality of the Spirit

The Holy Spirit does what persons do. For example, the Spirit
speaks (Acts 13:2), sends out workers (Acts 13:4), is tempted (Acts
5:9), is blasphemed (Matthew 12:31), and teaches (John 14:26).

"He" and not "it." We call the Holy Spirit "he" and "him" on
the authority of Scripture, for Jesus uses these personal pronouns when referring to the Spirit. In Greek there are three gender options for pronouns—masculine, feminine, and neuter.
According to Greek grammar, pronouns must match the gender
of the nouns to which they refer. In other words, if "Spirit"
(Greek *pneuma*), which is of neuter gender, is used with pronouns, they must also be neuter. So we should expect to find
something like this: "But when *it* [neuter pronoun in Greek], the
Spirit [neuter noun in Greek] of truth, comes." But we do not
find that in John 16:13! Rather, we find, "But when He [Greek
ekeinos, masculine personal pronoun], the Spirit [Greek *pneuma,*
neuter noun] of truth, comes." John breaks the rules of Greek
grammar! It is as if the apostle goes out of his way to show that
the Holy Spirit is a *person* and not an *impersonal* "it."

Another intercessor. Jesus comforts his disciples with these
words: "And I will ask the Father, and He will give to you another
Intercessor, in order that He might be with you forever" (John
14:16, my translation). Since Jesus is a person and an "intercessor" (or Comforter, Helper, Advocate; see 1 John 2:1), his calling
the Holy Spirit "another Intercessor" implies that the Spirit is a
person. Further, only a *person* can intercede for others. Just as

Jesus intercedes on behalf of his people to the Father (1 John 2:1), so does the Spirit (Romans 8:26–27).

The Deity and Work of the Spirit

The Holy Spirit is equal in nature and power with the Father and the Son. The deity of the Spirit is proved in Scripture within two general categories: (1) passages that equate the Spirit with God and (2) passages that speak of the Spirit's divine attributes.

Passages equating the Spirit with God. In the rebuke of Ananias in Acts 5:3–4, Peter equated lying to the Holy Spirit (v. 3) with lying to God (v. 4). In the discipline of biblical **exegesis,** this is known as "synonymous parallelism." Quite simply, the phrase "lied to the Holy Spirit" and "lied to God" are synonymous phrases, thus equating the Holy Spirit with God.

The Spirit and God are also parallel in a verse in the Gospel of Matthew. According to the words of Jesus in Matthew 28:19, believers are to be baptized "in the name of the Father and the Son and the Holy Spirit." The Holy Spirit is here placed on an equal plane with the Father and the Son; that is, all three persons are listed as sharing in the divine "name" (note that "name" is singular!).

Parity among the three persons is evident also in the writings of Paul. The apostle concludes his second letter to the believers in Corinth with these words: "The grace of the Lord Jesus Christ, and the love of God [the Father], and the fellowship of the Holy Spirit, be with you all" (2 Corinthians 13:14). Once again the Spirit is listed on equal par with the Son and the Father, as all three persons minister to the saints (Christians).

Passages teaching of the Spirit's divine attributes. Pneumatology, like **Christology,** has functional (what the Spirit does) and ontological (who the Spirit is) elements. We have seen that what Christ does implies who he is; it is the same with the Holy Spirit. Here too the functional implies the ontological. In the study of pneumatology, what the Spirit *does* is identified as "the work of the Spirit."

In John 14:16 Jesus says, "And I will ask the Father, and He will give you another Helper [the Holy Spirit], that He may be with you forever." I believe that the key ingredient in God's relationship with his people is the promise to be *with* them. This is known as the "divine presence." All throughout the Old Testament, *Yahweh* (the Hebrew word translated "LORD" in many modern translations) promises to be present with his people. Take, for example, Isaiah 43:5, where Yahweh states, "Do not fear, for I am with you." In John 14:16 Jesus is telling us that it is the Spirit who possesses the divine attribute of being *with* the people of God, an attribute that is true only of Yahweh!

The apostle Paul uses Old Testament language that starkly calls his readers back to the temple where God dwelled in a special way with his people (though God was also everywhere present). It is a standard Old Testament theme: God dwelled in the temple. Against this Old Testament background, Paul says to the Christians at Corinth: "Do you not know that your body is a temple of the Holy Spirit who is in you, whom you have from God, and that you are not your own?" (1 Corinthians 6:19). Paul's words ("your body is a temple of the Holy Spirit") teach us that the Holy Spirit is God *present* among and in his people!

Additionally, this verse, when it is coupled with 1 Corinthians 3:16, equates the Spirit with God. In 1 Corinthians 3:16 Paul states, "Do you not know that you are a temple of God?" The parallelism is clear: "temple of the Holy Spirit" (6:19) and "temple of God" (3:16).

What distinguishes God's people from the rest of the world is that God (by the Holy Spirit!) is *present* in the people, both individually and collectively as the one body of Christ. Therefore what the Spirit *does* (the divine presence; functional) implies who the Spirit *is* (God; ontological).

The Scripture assigns several other divine attributes to the Holy Spirit. These attributes, as those above, belong only to God. The Spirit is eternal (Hebrews 9:14), omniscient (knows all things; 1 Corinthians 2:11), omnipresent (everywhere present; Psalm 139:7), and sovereign and omnipotent (controls all things and is all-powerful; Luke 1:35; John 16:8; 1 Corinthians 12:11). Again, these functional attributes of the Holy Spirit imply who the Spirit is ontologically. If the Holy Spirit exists eternally, exercises infinite knowledge, exists everywhere at all times, and is in control of all things everywhere at all times, then the Spirit is God. These functions can belong to no one but God.

Further work of the Spirit. Two important aspects of the work of God the Holy Spirit are seen in creation and in formation of the Scriptures. We will look into these in some depth and then follow with a brief listing of further works of the Spirit.

The Spirit's work in the creation of all things is most clearly evidenced in Genesis 1:2–3. We can take the second half of verse 2 and place it with verse 3: "The Spirit of God was moving over the surface of the waters. Then God said, 'Let there be light'; and there was light." There is an immediate connection here. That is to say, the Holy Spirit's activity ("moving" or "hovering") in verse 2 cannot be separated from the act of creating in verse 3 ("Then God said")! The same connection can be seen juxtaposing the second half of verse 2 and verses 4–31. In other words, the Holy Spirit is active in *all* the creation account of Genesis 1.

In addition to a role in creation, the Holy Spirit had a role in the formation of God's Word. Indeed, when Paul instructed Timothy that "all Scripture is inspired by God" (2 Timothy 3:16), he was not eliminating the Holy Spirit's role in this process. We should view "inspired" as meaning "God-breathed." That being so, it reminds us of the creative act of God in "breathing" into Adam "the breath of life" (Genesis 2:7).

In the light of other passages and themes in the Bible, we gather that the Holy Spirit was quite active in the God-breathing (the creating) of Scripture. For example, Peter states that in Old Testament times, *"men moved by the Holy Spirit spoke from God"* (2 Peter 1:21, emphasis added). Indeed, all through the Old Testament the Spirit speaks through his servants. And Jesus states that the apostles' ministry of proclaiming Christ (and also their writings!) was going to be the result of the Holy Spirit's reminding them of all that Jesus had said to them (John 14:26). We should conclude, then, that implicit in the statement "God gave us the Bible" is the role of God the Holy Spirit in the whole process.

The Holy Spirit's work is not limited to creation and the formation of Scripture. We learn from Scripture that the Spirit acts distinctively in the world. First, the Holy Spirit convicts the world of sin, righteousness, and judgment (John 16:8). Second, the Spirit empowers the disciples for the preaching of the gospel (Acts 1:8). From this, we gather that the Spirit will do the same for us as we go forth to share the gospel with those around us (read Peter's sermon and the results on the day of Pentecost; Acts 2:14–47). Third, the Spirit takes the lead in the Trinity in the regeneration (making new, born again) of God's people (John 3:3,5–6). Fourth, the Holy Spirit teaches believers (John 15:26). A large part of this is done through the Spirit's leading us to study God's Word (both privately and in church settings) and in our prayer time (which includes our listening for what the Spirit might have to say!). Fifth, the Holy Spirit is our intercessor. That is, the Spirit intercedes for us when we pray and gives us the words to pray when we do not know how to pray (Romans 8:26–27). Finally, the Spirit brings the Christian into conformity with God's will and is in the process of making us holy, or sanctifying us (that is, maturing us in knowledge of Christ and turning us into the servants God wants us to be; more on this in chap. 8).

For Discussion

1. On what authority do we refer to the Spirit as "he" and "him"? What would be lost by referring to the Spirit as "it"?

2. In pneumatology, how does the functional imply the ontological? Give some biblical examples of this.

3. Think of some of the things that the Holy Spirit does. How are they important to us?

 **Meditation**

You Are a Temple!

Do you not know that your body is a temple of the Holy Spirit who is in you? (1 Corinthians 6:19)

The temple we read about in the Old Testament was the place where God dwelled. In the temple was the divine presence of the

Lord. Now there is no need for that temple. Paul says that each one of us is a temple in which God the Holy Spirit dwells.

Even as I write this, I am amazed. *God* dwells in me! As you read this, are you amazed at the thought of that for yourself? When we consider the specks of dust that we are in the grand scheme of things, how truly stupendous it is that God has chosen to dwell in each of us.

When you go to work tomorrow, or when you stay at home with the kids, when you do whatever it is that you do tomorrow, practice the realization that those with whom you come into contact are coming into contact with the presence of God in you. What does that mean for us? It means many things. One that comes immediately to mind is that I want to be counted worthy of that privilege. I want those people to see the true and living God in me. I want people to see that I "have been bought with a price" and that I "therefore glorify God in . . . [my] body," as Paul says in 1 Corinthians 6:20. In these people's presence, I want them to see *the* presence.

Dear and precious Holy Spirit, allow others to see you in me. For Jesus' sake. Amen.

PART TWO

The Work
of Christ

4

The Birth, Life, and Death of Christ

⊕

THINK OF SOME PEOPLE WHOM YOU LOVE AND CHERISH BEYOND measure. When we love and cherish people, we have an intimate relationship with them. We also know things about them. But it does not stop there. It seems quite natural that we seek to know more about the ones we love and cherish.

For those of us who claim to love the Lord Jesus Christ, what should characterize our relationship with him is seeking to know all that we can about him. And in making for himself a people, Jesus has secured for them the means of knowing more about him. He has revealed himself to us in the Bible.

The Basics

In this chapter we will learn more about Jesus, specifically his birth, life, and death. In doing so, and in holding these things in our hearts, we will be blessed beyond measure.

The Virgin Birth

In chapter 2 we learned that Jesus Christ existed from all eternity as the Son of God (God the Son). In other words, before his birth on earth as the God-man, Jesus existed eternally in the past as the "Word" (remember that the Word is a **person,** not some impersonal thing). The virgin birth is that aspect of **Christology** in which the Word, the second person of the Trinity, the Son of God, is conceived and born as a full human being in the womb of the virgin Mary.

Isaiah 7:14. When Jesus was conceived and born, it was in fulfillment of an Old Testament prophecy. The prophet Isaiah spoke these words: "Therefore the Lord Himself will give you a sign: Behold, a virgin will be with child and bear a son, and she will call His name Immanuel" (Isaiah 7:14). In the New Testament, Matthew cites Isaiah 7:14 as fulfilled with the conception and birth of Jesus Christ (Matthew 1:23).

Matthew 1:18. Matthew himself states, "Now the birth of Jesus Christ was as follows. When his mother Mary had been betrothed to Joseph, before they came together she was found to be with child by the Holy Spirit." Two things are significant in this statement. First, the Holy Spirit was the direct agent of the conception of Jesus (*"by* the Holy Spirit"). Second, the conception took place while Mary was still a virgin. This is the meaning of "before they [that is, Mary and Joseph] came together."

Luke 1:35. Luke specifically names Mary as being a virgin. In Luke 1:26–27 we read that "the angel Gabriel was sent from God . . . to a virgin . . . and the virgin's name was Mary." Gabriel announces to Mary that she is going to bear a son, Jesus, and that he "will be called the Son of the Most High" (vv. 31–32).

Mary then asks Gabriel, "How can this be, since I am a virgin?" (v. 34). The angel answers in verse 35, "The Holy Spirit will come upon you, and the power of the Most High will overshadow you." This passage, then, shows (1) that Mary was a virgin at the time of the conception and birth and (2) that the Holy Spirit was the direct cause of the conception.

The Life of Christ

When **Christian** theologians speak of "the life of Christ," they do so knowing full well that he existed eternally prior to his **incarnation** and that he exists even now as the resurrected and exalted God-man. The life of Christ in this sense encompasses all eternity. But usually the phrase "the life of Christ" refers to what Jesus did when he walked the earth—his birth, death, resurrection, and ascension. Here, however, I want to focus on the *actual life* Jesus lived between his birth and death. This is what I mean by "the life of Christ."

In one sense, it is the life that Jesus *lived* that makes his death on the cross so wonderfully able to save us from our sins. In this sense, *who* is on the cross is the issue. The sacrifice offered for sin must be totally blameless, "without blemish." We see this over and over again in the Old Testament.

In Exodus 12:5 the LORD commands Moses about the sacrifice of a lamb: "Your lamb shall be an unblemished male a year old." What is the meaning of this? It is to underscore the truth that the LORD requires a sacrifice without any defect at all. This command is first and foremost a testimony to the nature of the LORD. Nothing short of perfection will satisfy him.

In order to meet the requirements of sacrifice for the holy and perfect God, the life of Christ must be perfect. And his life was just that—perfect! John the Baptist calls upon the above Old Testament theme when he sees Jesus for the first time: "Behold, the Lamb of God who takes away the sin of the world!" (John 1:29). Peter as well refers to Christ "as of a lamb unblemished and spotless" (1 Peter 1:19).

"Without blemish" has to do largely with the obedience of Christ. This may surprise some, for how can we speak of the obedience of one who is himself God? In other words, to whom could God ever be obedient? The answer lies in Christ's humanity. As a full human, Jesus was obedient to the Father, living out what we ourselves cannot do. Jesus was morally perfect. Hebrews 4:15 says that Jesus was "tempted in all things as we are, yet without sin." As a human being, Jesus "learned obedience" (Hebrews 5:8). And Paul takes all this and points to its marvelous result: "Even so through the obedience of the One [Jesus] the many will be made righteous" (Romans 5:19). I will have more to say about this later (see chap. 7). For now it is important to note that we as Christians have been saved because Christ lived a perfect life for us by the power and ministry of God the Holy Spirit! It is in this sense that the *life* of Christ is as important as his *death*.

The Death of Christ

The crucifixion of Jesus was agonizing and slow. He was executed as common criminals were executed—by torture on a cross. He was mocked, spit upon, and beaten (Matthew 27:27–31). Then the sinless Lord of glory spent hours hanging on the cross, shedding his precious blood.

Jesus *really* died: "But coming to Jesus, when they saw that He was already dead, they did not break His legs" (John 19:33). Because Jesus was a real and full human being, and was crucified, he died a real death. And, as we shall see in our next chapter, that death meant something far beyond anything we could imagine.

For Discussion

1. Who was the direct cause of the conception of Jesus?

2. Did the conception of Jesus take place in the womb of the virgin Mary?

3. How is the life of Jesus important for the meaning of his crucifixion? In other words, why did Jesus lead a perfect life of obedience to the Father in the power of the Holy Spirit?

4. Why is it important that Jesus died a real death?

Beyond the Basics

The Virgin Birth

The eternal *logos* (the Word) became flesh in the womb of the virgin Mary by the Holy Spirit. Two verses aid us in this understanding.

John 1:14. The "Word" of John 1:1, that is, Jesus in his **preincarnate** state, became a man: "And the Word became flesh, and dwelt among us" (1:14). Though Jesus always existed as God the Son, John says his flesh "became."

In the Incarnation we have two natures—God and man—in the one person of Jesus Christ. His God nature always existed, but his flesh had a beginning in time. John 1:14 is not teaching that the Word *changed* into a man, meaning that his deity was gone. Rather, it teaches that the Word's flesh came into existence—his flesh "became." In other words, the eternal Word joined to himself a full human nature "and dwelt among us."

Matthew 1:18. Mary conceived Jesus by a direct act of the Holy Spirit. Matthew 1:18 states that "she was found to be with child *by* the Holy Spirit" (emphasis added). Some translations read "*of* the Holy Spirit," but the meaning is nonetheless the same. The Greek preposition from which we get "by" or "of" is *ek*. It is a preposition denoting *direct agency*. In other words, the Holy Spirit is the *means by which* the virgin conception took place. Therefore, on the basis of John 1:14 and Matthew 1:18, Christians believe that the eternal *logos* (the Word) became flesh in the womb of the virgin Mary by the Holy Spirit.

Implications of the virgin conception and birth. For the following reasons, it is important that we affirm the virgin birth. First, the virgin birth is the instrument that the triune God chose to bring the eternal Son of God into the world. It thus is the instrument of the Incarnation. Second, the virgin birth is the vehicle used to bring the Son of God into the world to save sinners. Finally, we must never believe that Jesus became the Son of God (God the Son) at his incarnation, for he always was the Son of God. Rather, the eternal God the Son became the *God-man* at the moment of the virgin conception.

The Life of Christ

"Life of Christ" in the context of this book refers to the life Jesus led between his birth and death (though certainly one can place his virgin birth, death, resurrection, and ascension in this category). Perhaps the most important of all aspects of the life of Christ was his righteousness. We earlier learned that Christ was perfect and sinless and that because of this he was called "the Lamb of God who takes away the sin of the world" (John 1:29). The concept of Christ's righteousness is linked with this.

What is righteousness? Because Jesus is the perfect, sinless Lamb of God, he is called "Jesus Christ the righteous" (1 John 2:1). But what does this mean? First of all, only God is inherently righteous. We know this implicitly from the apostle Paul, who wrote, "THERE IS NONE RIGHTEOUS, NOT EVEN ONE" (Romans 3:10). Paul means to say that no one of us is righteous in and of ourselves.

The word "righteous" has many shades of meaning. When we think of God, we think of superlatives such as perfect, holy, just, and good. So I would define righteousness as "those qualities of perfection that belong to God." Christ, then, is righteous, and what characterized his life was righteousness.

In what way was Christ righteous? Jesus was righteous in many ways, but one in particular really stands out. The theme is basically this: What Adam and the nation of Israel did not do, Jesus did.

Let us take Adam. Simply put, Adam gave in to temptation as he directly broke the command of God. Adam was not to eat of the tree of the knowledge of good and evil (Genesis 2:17). But he did (Genesis 3:6). Jesus, however, was tempted in every way just as we (and Adam) are, but he sinned not (Hebrews 4:15). This is one reason why Jesus is called the *last* Adam (1 Corinthians 15:45) and the *second* Adam (1 Corinthians 15:47).

As for Israel, God's people gave in to multiple temptations and broke the commands of God. For example, Israel was led by God into the wilderness to be tempted for forty years (Deuteronomy 8:2). But Israel failed. Jesus, however, "was led up by the Spirit into the wilderness to be tempted by the devil. And after he had fasted forty days and forty nights, He then became hungry" (Matthew 4:1–2). But Jesus did not give in to the temptations of the devil. The parallel of the forty years of Israel's wilderness temptations and the forty days of Christ's wilderness temptations is no coincidence. What Israel failed to do, Christ did!

It is precisely these righteous acts (among others) of Christ that testify to his intrinsic, his essential, righteousness. We will see later, when we examine salvation, that it is this righteousness of Christ that the Father pronounces (declares) upon those who have faith in his Son. Christ is the Israel that did not fail, and since we, as Christians, are in Christ, it is no wonder, then, that we are called "Israel"!

The Death of Christ

Jesus' death was not some hoax, as some say. His death was not an illusion, as others say. Some even believe that Jesus was simply rendered unconscious on the cross, taken down, and "buried" in a staged ceremony. But Christians affirm the reality of Jesus' death. Certainly there are negative implications if he did not die.

First, if any of the above deceptions would be true, then Jesus failed to fulfill the predetermined plan of the Father. Peter states that Jesus was "delivered up by the predetermined plan and foreknowledge of God" (Acts 2:23). If Jesus failed in this, then he was not obedient to the will of the Father. If Jesus was not obedient to the Father's will, then he was not perfect. If he was not perfect, his death means nothing (for only a perfect sacrifice is acceptable). No, Jesus' death was real (John 19:33).

Second, if Jesus did not die, there would be no "New Testament." The word "testament" means **"covenant."** A *covenant* is a mutual agreement between two or more parties. God is the maker and provider of the covenant of **redemption** (see chap. 7) for his people, but there would be no new covenant of redemption if Jesus did not live a perfect life and die. In the book of Hebrews we are told, "For where a covenant is, there must of necessity be the death of the one who made it" (9:16).

What is so sobering to us, so humbling, and what should make every Christian cry tears of joy, is that because of this death, we have life. Pause for a moment to think as you read this: the irony, no, the grace of it all, is that Jesus did not deserve death. "The wages of sin," says the Bible, "is death" (Romans 6:23). Yet Jesus died. The Creator of the universe died. He created the very wood upon which he was crucified. He fashioned out of nothing the nails that penetrated his hands and feet. He created the very soldiers who mocked him and spit upon him and beat him. He created them for this very purpose.

But Jesus' action does not stop here. The next chapter explains the reason for the death of the sinless Lamb of God and the eternal life we have because of it.

For Discussion

1. Did Jesus become the Son of God at the moment of the virgin conception or birth?

2. What was the vehicle by which the eternal Son of God joined with his full deity a full human nature?

3. If Jesus did not die, there would be no new covenant. Why is the death of Christ important to the new covenant?

4. In his life, Jesus did what Adam and Israel did not do—he obeyed God the Father. Discuss how this relates to salvation.

 Meditation

Conceived and Born

When his mother Mary had been betrothed to Joseph, before they came together she was found to be with child by the Holy Spirit. (Matthew 1:18)

Though we must never forget that God's Son existed eternally, equally we must never lose sight of the fact that the Son of God took upon himself full humanity in the womb of the virgin. Here is a most important truth: with the virgin conception and birth, the Son of God had taken on a new and different type of existence.

Everything that we experienced in the womb, from conception to development, this child to be called Jesus experienced by virtue of his complete humanity. And, once born, Jesus grew and developed just as true humans do. What set him apart from all humans, though, was that he lived the only perfect and righteous life in the history of the world. Further, he died for the sins of countless numbers of his people.

It is beyond our fullest comprehension. We must stand in awe of this. The eternal Word who spoke the worlds into existence now lies silent in the womb. The almighty hands that fashioned the universe and that hold it together are now the hands of a baby boy. The innocent babe in the manger, unable yet to utter a word, will one day come as judge of the living and the dead.

Thank you, Father, for sending your Son to be born of the virgin by your Holy Spirit. In the hours to come, help us to reflect on the conception and birth of the Son of God. Help us to ask ourselves what this event means for our salvation. In the name of him who came to be one of us. Amen.

5

The Atonement of Christ

✛

CHRISTIAN THEOLOGY IS LIKE A GARMENT—THE THREADS OF **doctrine** are all tied together. Consequently, if in our theology one essential doctrine is off base, the whole system suffers. The birth, life, and death of Christ are the basis of his atonement, resurrection, and ascension. In other words, without Jesus' becoming a man, living a perfect life, and dying a real death, there would be no atonement, resurrection, and ascension.

The Basics

We continue with the work of Christ, focusing on his atonement for sin. In the last chapter we learned that Jesus' birth, life, and death are necessary to bring about the **redemption** of God's people. The same is said of the Atonement.

Atonement as Fundamental

The Atonement is a fundamental Christian doctrine. The general meaning is "covering." The death of Christ is a death of atonement and as such marks the beginning of the new **covenant** agreement between God and God's people. In Christ's death, God reconciles us to himself (2 Corinthians 5:19; see **reconciliation** in the glossary).

God purposed that the atonement of Christ would involve the shedding of blood. Thus, atonement occurs when blood is shed in order to "cover" (forgive) the guilty party's sin. This is why the writer of Hebrews says, "Without the shedding of blood there is no forgiveness" (9:22). The writer of Hebrews was certainly well acquainted with the Old Testament, where we first find the concept of the shedding of blood for atonement.

Why atonement? Why must there be atonement, the shedding of blood? It is quite simple. God is holy and just, and we are sinners; therefore, a payment for sin must be made. Some say God *could have* chosen another way. Some have even suggested that God could have just "zapped" us into being Christians. But God didn't. The reason is because God is just, perfect, and holy. It would not be justice for God to pass over sin without some sacrifice. God cannot let sin go without exercising some form of judgment.

And judge God did! It all started with the first sin—that of Adam and Eve. Adam and Eve disobeyed the command of God not to eat of the fruit of the tree of the knowledge of good and evil. They immediately became sinners, guilty of breaking God's law. Yet God is so gracious that immediately upon declaring judgment for their sin, God provided "garments of skin," coverings, for them (Genesis 3:21). We gather from this that there had to be a sacrifice, a shedding of the blood of animals, to provide these garments for Adam and Eve.

Genesis 3 sets the stage for the rest of the Old Testament, especially the first five books written by Moses (called "the Pentateuch"). You and I cannot read the Old Testament without running squarely into the concept of atonement provided by God through the shedding of blood (see, for example, Leviticus 4:3–5). As the Lord stated through Moses concerning blood, "I have given it to you on the altar to make atonement" (Leviticus 17:11).

When atonement is made, God does not condemn the guilty who believe in the divine provision of atonement. One of the greatest examples of this occurs in Exodus 11–12, when God "passes over" the houses of faithful followers.

God's judgment is pronounced upon Egypt because Pharaoh opposed God's purpose to free the Israelites from slavery. This judgment culminates with the promise of God to slay all the firstborn children of the land (Exodus 11:4–5). The LORD, however, provides a way for Israel to escape this awesome judgment. Such escape is through the blood of the "passover lamb." God commands that each household take an unblemished lamb, slay it, and place the blood "on the two doorposts and on the lintel of the houses in which they eat it" (Exodus 12:7). God then says, "When I see the blood I will pass over you, and no plague will befall you to destroy you" (v. 13).

Christ's atonement. The above examples from the Old Testament serve ultimately to point to Jesus Christ's blood atonement on the cross. In all these examples *something else,* instead of the guilty, is being sacrificed. In the Exodus account, it was a lamb. The lamb was killed, and its blood was shed *for* God's people. This becomes vital in our understanding of Christ's atonement on the cross.

The Old Testament theme of sacrificing a lamb without blemish so that its blood may be offered up before the LORD in order to save the people from condemnation is what God ordained to point to Christ. Jesus is called "the Lamb of God who takes away the sin of the world" (John 1:29). Jesus is the Lamb without blemish, the one who is without sin (1 Peter 1:19; Hebrews 4:15), whose blood was shed (Mark 14:24) so that God would "pass over" us, not dealing the wrath we so richly and justly deserve.

Thankfully, we see God's glory and grace in that Jesus died for our sins in our place. This is the *substitution* aspect of the Atonement, an aspect we must never forget. Paul says, "Christ died for us" (Romans 5:8). And who are "us"? Paul tells us—"the ungodly" (Romans 5:6). There can be no greater story than this: The one who knew no sin was made to be the sin offering on our behalf, that we might become the righteousness of God (2 Corinthians 5:21).

Rejoice. Christ died for you!

For Discussion

1. What is the general meaning of "atonement"?

2. Does atonement require the shedding of blood? Why?

3. Do all the "substitute" sacrifices of the Old Testament point to Christ?

4. Atonement comes with the sacrifice of an "unblemished" substitute for the sins of the people. Discuss the importance of substitution as it relates to salvation.

Beyond the Basics

Why must there be atonement for sin? To answer this question in more detail, we must begin with the basic premise that all theology starts with God. So understanding the doctrine of the Atonement necessitates first learning (1) who and what God is, (2) who and what humanity is, and (3) what is therefore required of humanity. Thereafter we will delve into different shades of meaning of the word "atonement," particularly in the context of how these meanings apply to Christ.

God

Perfectly and infinitely holy, just, righteous, and good, God is all these in a way well beyond our comprehension. With God there is no imperfection. Also, God is love. It is no wonder that the phrase "God is love" appears in the Bible in the context of the atonement of Christ: "The one who does not love does not know God, for God is love. . . . In this is love, not that we loved God, but that He loved us and sent His Son to be the propitiation for our sins" (1 John 4:8,10).

Notice that John's theology starts with God! God *first loved us* and sent the Son as atonement for the sins of God's people. God did not love us because we loved God. We did not love God first. No, God initiated the whole process for his own glory! Thus God must always be at the head and center of the Atonement.

Humanity

Humanity is sinful and wretched. Do we fully grasp that point? The hymn we sing says it all: "Amazing grace, how sweet the sound, That saved a wretch like me." In contrast, the popular message today is that we are basically good. But if our theology starts with the God of the Bible (thereby defining "good" by what God is) and continues on in honest fashion to interpret the facts of what we are, we can come to no other conclusion than that we are sinful and wretched.

Jesus tells us what we are. He says that "out of the heart come evil thoughts, murders, adulteries, fornications, thefts, false witness, slanders" (Matthew 15:19). Can anyone of us say we are not guilty of these?

What, Then, Is Required?

Based on what he knew of God's nature and humanity's nature, Paul stated, "The wages of sin is death" (Romans 6:23). Quite simply, all humanity deserves to die. We deserve to die because God is just. God's self-revelation tells us what we are and what we deserve.

In spite of our sin, however, God desires eternal life for us because God is love. The Deity does this for glory. Paul states that God makes known the riches of the divine glory upon vessels (Christians) of mercy (Romans 9:23). God saves us, Paul says, "to the praise of His glory" (Ephesians 1:14). And why not, for only God is worthy of it!

It is with the atonement of Christ's shed blood that God saves (Ephesians 1:7), for "without shedding of blood there is no forgiveness" (Hebrews 9:22). Our forgiveness (God's not condemning us because of our sins) comes because our sins have been covered by Christ's atonement. Indeed, Christ's atonement was *substitutionary;* that is, Christ died *for* us.

John teaches us that Jesus "is the propitiation for our sins" (1 John 2:2). **Propitiation** is the taking away of the divine wrath of God, which is the Deity's anger against sin and eternal act of judgment against sinners. Thankfully, Paul says, "we shall be saved from the wrath of God through Him [Jesus]" (Romans 5:9). Paul thus calls our attention to both the propitiatory ("saved from the wrath of God") and the substitutionary ("through Him") aspects of the atonement of Christ.

The Atonement of Jesus Alone

Why can atonement be made by Jesus alone? Here is the situation: because of divine justice, God requires humanity to pay the penalty for sins. Now, how can God's justice be satisfied without wiping out the entire human race? Further, how is it that God does it all? In other words, how does God both satisfy divine justice *and* pay for our sins?

The answer is Jesus. Remember the two natures of Christ Jesus, who is both God and man! Because Jesus is God the Son, God therefore gives of himself to pay for our sins. And because Jesus is fully human, he is able to take the place of human beings in that payment. Two passages buttress these two points and lend scriptural proof to the statement that "God does it all." The first talks about the humanity of Christ.

Hebrews 2:17. This great passage teaches that Jesus must be a real and complete human being if his sacrifice is to apply to his people. We read, "Therefore, He had to be made like His brethren in all things *(kata panta),* that He might become a merciful and faithful high priest in things pertaining to God, to make propitiation for the sins of the people."

Jesus *had* to be made like us "in every respect" (another translation of the Greek *kata panta*) in order to atone for the sins of his people. In other words, if Jesus did not possess, let's say, a human spirit, then our spirits would not be saved. God requires humanity to pay the price for sin. This requirement is met in Jesus.

Genesis 15:17. This second passage points to Jesus as God paying the penalty for sin. In it Abram (later called Abraham) receives a vision from the LORD. Genesis 15:17 reads, "And it came about when the sun had set, that it was very dark, and behold, there appeared a smoking oven and a flaming torch which passed between these pieces [of the animals that were cut in two; see vv. 9–10]." A little ancient Near Eastern historical and cultural background is necessary for an understanding and appreciation of this amazing passage. Whenever a treaty (or covenant) was made between two parties (a ruling party and a weaker party), some sacrificial victim was cut in two pieces. The weaker party (who was to come under the authority of the ruling party) would then pass between the pieces, saying something to this effect: "Should I break our treaty, let this happen to me." (A good study Bible or commentary on this passage will give you further information on this tradition.)

In Genesis 15 the smoking oven and flaming torch are the presence of God. Obviously the LORD is here establishing a covenant with Abram. The LORD is the ruling party, and Abram is the party subject to the LORD. Now here is what is so incredible—Abram should be the one passing between the pieces! Instead, it is the LORD who does so. The LORD is saying, "If the covenant should be broken, let this happen to me." The true and living God is offering to pay the awful price if the covenant is broken! This is truly remarkable because the LORD, of course, knew who could not break it (God) and who would (humanity). This was a foreshadowing of what was going to happen to our Lord Jesus Christ. His body was sacrificed, even though we are the guilty ones.

Can you fathom such love? I cannot. I can only weep with thankfulness when I contemplate such an act by our gracious God.

For Discussion

1. Does the theology of the Atonement start with God? Why?

2. Why is there a need for atonement?

3. Discuss the various shades of meaning of the Atonement.

4. In the Atonement, how is it that God does it all? In other words, how is that God both paid the price and remained just?

✚ **Meditation**

Jesus Had to Be Fully Human

Therefore, he had to be made like his brethren in all things, that he might become a merciful and faithful high priest in things pertaining to God, to make propitiation for the sins of the people. (Hebrews 2:17)

Jesus' atonement for the sins of his people could not have occurred, says the writer of Hebrews, had he not been fully human. Jesus, in order to redeem us fully, redeem every part of our makeup as human beings (body, soul, and spirit), had to be made like us "in all things," or "in every respect." He was himself fully human, just as we are, yet, of course, without sin (Hebrews 4:15).

Had Jesus not come, the only way to heaven for us would be to live a perfect life. But because of sin, no one—not one—is righteous enough to do so. Thus, we deserve only the wrath of God. However, God in every respect became one of us to live that perfect life and sacrifice himself, submitting to God's wrath. Such love. Such grace.

There have been instances in which someone chose to die in order that someone else might live. Perhaps we know someone who sacrificed life and limb like this. At the very least we all have heard stories about such things happening. Though these acts of bravery and sacrifice allow others to live, and should be respected and applauded, do they bring with them *eternal* life? What's more, do they bring eternal life to millions?

Thank you, Father, that it pleased you to make your Son the atonement for our sins. Such love, such grace, can only be true of you. We praise you for Jesus. We thank you that you sent him to become like us in every respect and that he has brought us eternal life. In Jesus' name. Amen.

6

The Resurrection and Ascension of Christ

✚

"HE LIVES, HE LIVES, CHRIST JESUS LIVES TODAY!" AROUND Eastertime you will hear this hymn as **Christians** sing it to celebrate Christ's resurrection. Christians believe Jesus was raised from the dead. He was resurrected after dying a real death on the cross. Christians also believe that Jesus ascended to the right hand of the Father after his resurrection.

But what do we mean when we affirm that Jesus rose from the dead? Was Jesus' body raised, or was it only his spirit? Also, was Jesus' ascension spiritual or physical in nature? Further, since his resurrection from the dead and his ascension to the Father, what does Jesus *do?*

The Basics

The resurrection and ascension of Jesus are fundamental Christian beliefs for many reasons. One reason answers the question, "Why should I be a Christian?"

The Importance of the Resurrection

In 1 Corinthians 15:14 Paul pretty much says that if Christ is not raised from the dead, Christianity is useless: "If Christ has not been raised, then our preaching is vain, your faith also is vain." If Christ is not raised, cancel Easter! All of this is worthless.

The marvelous fact, however, is that Christ *did* rise from the dead. Therefore our preaching is not in vain—what we tell others about Jesus is eternally significant. And our faith is not in vain. What we as Christians believe is eternally significant.

A Physical Resurrection

Some believe that Jesus' spirit alone was raised. Others believe that only Jesus' thinking was raised from dead thoughts. Still others say that Jesus was a mere man who died and stayed dead. What is the orthodox Christian position (see **orthodoxy** in the glossary)? And why do we believe it?

The orthodox Christian position is that Jesus' resurrection was a *bodily* one, and we believe it because the Bible teaches it. But Christians must not only affirm that Christ's resurrection was bodily; we must also affirm that the same body that died on the cross was raised.

John 2:19 records Jesus as saying, "Destroy this temple, and in three days I will raise it up." The Jews misunderstood him, thinking that he was talking of the temple, the actual building itself (v. 20). But John then tells us what Jesus meant: "He was speaking of the temple of His body" (v. 21). Jesus used "this temple" to signify the body he had when he was talking to the Jews. John knew this and has passed that knowledge on to us. This is why we believe that Jesus' resurrection was bodily and that *the same body* that died on the cross was raised from the dead.

A Physical Ascension

After staying awhile with his disciples in his resurrected state, Jesus *ascended* into heaven to the right hand of the Father. His ascension was also bodily. After Jesus appeared to his disciples for the last time, he was taken up into heaven on a cloud (Acts 1:9–11).

Scripture also tells us that Jesus ascended to "the right hand of God [the Father]" (Romans 8:34). In ancient times, to sit at someone's right hand was to affirm to all that you shared in the authority of the one next to whom you sat. Thus, when the biblical writers state that Jesus is "at the right hand of God," they mean to say that Jesus has the authority of God.

The Importance of the Ascension

The Ascension was necessary if Jesus was to go and prepare a place in heaven for his people (John 14:2–3). Part of this preparation involves what Jesus *now does* as he is seated at the right hand of the Father.

By virtue of both his humanity and deity, Jesus is able to be our "go-between." In other words, he mediates between the Father and us. In the Old Testament the high priest went to God on behalf of the people and offered sacrifices to God for their sins. Jesus is the ultimate fulfillment of the role of high priest, and consequently there is no need for any other to be our mediator. Paul tells us this: "For there is one God, and one mediator also between God and men, the man Christ Jesus" (1 Timothy 2:5).

Hebrews 2:17 calls Jesus the "faithful high priest." As such, he is able to offer sacrifice for the people, making atonement for sins (2:17). The wonderful thing about this is that Jesus himself is the sacrifice that was offered "once" (Hebrews 9:28). Once and that's it! There is no need to repeat the sacrifice for sins. Jesus did it once for all. And since he did it once for all, his mediating/high priestly role cannot be shared with another. As the writer of Hebrews claims, Jesus "holds His priesthood permanently" (7:24).

For Discussion

1. What are the consequences if Christ did not rise from the dead?

2. Christ's resurrection was a bodily resurrection, and Christ's ascension was a bodily ascension. Why are the *bodily* resurrection and the *bodily* ascension important?

Beyond the Basics

If Christ is not raised from the dead, Paul says, our preaching and our faith are in vain (1 Corinthians 15:14). Paul, however, does not stop there.

The Importance of the Resurrection

Paul exclaims as well that if Christ did not rise from the dead, "you are still in your sins" (1 Corinthians 15:17). With no resurrection, there is no victory over sin and its consequence—death. But with the reality of the resurrection, "DEATH," Paul says, "IS SWALLOWED UP in victory" (1 Corinthians 15:54). This "victory," of course, must be the resurrection since Paul spends all of 1 Corinthians 15 talking about it.

So far we have explored the consequences of there being no resurrection of Jesus. Now I want to share with you the consequence of denying it.

The consequence of denying the resurrection. There are many ways to deny the resurrection of Christ. For example, one can deny that it ever happened. Or one can say that it did happen but redefine what "resurrection" means. Some believe that Jesus' spirit alone was raised. Others define Jesus' resurrection as an elevating of his thinking.

The consequence of these forms of denial is that such persons are not Christians. This is a difficult thing to say, but it is nonetheless true, for the Bible says so. Just as the Scripture says that someone intently denying Christ's deity cannot be a Christian (John 8:24), it says that anyone denying his *bodily* resurrection cannot be a Christian. A passage in Romans drives home both these points.

Perhaps you've shared Romans 10:9 with those you've evangelized. Here Paul states, "If you confess with your mouth Jesus as Lord, and believe in your heart that God raised Him from the dead, you shall be saved." "Lord" means "Yahweh"—the LORD, the true and living God. Just four verses later, Paul again uses "Lord," which refers back to Jesus as Lord in verse 9, as he quotes Joel 2:32: "WHOEVER WILL CALL UPON THE NAME OF THE LORD [Hebrew *Yahweh*] WILL BE SAVED." So, one must confess Jesus as Yahweh (God) to be saved and must also believe "that God raised Him from the dead." How was Jesus raised? *Bodily.* That is, the same body that died on the cross was raised. One must believe this to be saved.

Further evidence of Christ's bodily resurrection. In addition to John 2:19–21, we add two other passages to the biblical evidence for the bodily resurrection of Jesus: John 20:24–27 and Luke 24:36–39.

The nickname "doubting Thomas" unfortunately focuses only on the initial response of the disciple as reported in the Gospel of John. Days later he no longer doubted! In response to the disciples who told Thomas, "We have seen the Lord," Thomas said, "Unless I shall see in His hands the imprint of the nails, and put my finger into the place of the nails, and put my hand into His side, I will not believe" (v. 25). Eight days later all the disciples were together again. Jesus appears and says to Thomas, "Reach here and put your finger, and see My hands; and reach here your hand, and put it into My side" (v. 27). Thomas then believes and confesses Jesus as Lord and God (v. 28).

The point for our purpose is that Jesus' resurrection was a physical one. Jesus' appeal to Thomas to touch the wounds in his body suggests that it was the same body that was crucified and had died (fulfilling his earlier prediction in John 2:19).

According to the Gospel of Luke, Jesus' disciples were gathered, and Jesus "Himself stood in their midst" (24:36). It seems that Luke is careful to emphasize that it was "He [Jesus] Himself" because they were "frightened and thought that they were seeing a spirit" (v. 37). Jesus comforts them, showing them his hands and his feet, saying, "A spirit does not have flesh and bones as you see that I have" (v. 39). Later, Jesus even ate something in their sight (vv. 42–43).

The Ascension

The bodily ascension of Christ, his going up into heaven to the right hand of the Father, is his exaltation.

Christ's exaltation. The "exaltation" of Christ means his enthronement as King of kings and Lord of lords. Jesus is the enthroned Lord of glory, the exalted King of glory. He comes to his throne as the almighty God the Son, the sovereign judge of the universe. All this happened *after* Jesus' resurrection and *at* his ascension. Of course, there is a sense in which Jesus in his **preexistence** was exalted with the Father. Jesus himself says that he had glory with the Father "before the world was" (John 17:5). So in what sense is Jesus exalted at his ascension?

We must first note that Jesus *was* exalted to the right hand of God after his resurrection. Peter preached, "This Jesus God raised up again, to which we are all witnesses." He continues, "Therefore having been exalted to the right hand of God" (Acts 2:32–33). Furthermore, at his ascension Jesus is exalted as the now resurrected and glorified God-man. You see, even though Jesus had exaltation before his **incarnation** (as we saw in John 17:5), he did not have that *as man*. It is in this sense that Jesus is exalted after his resurrection. In the preexistence Jesus was not a man, so therefore his exaltation after the resurrection takes on a new significance. The New Testament writers (such as Peter above) pick up on this new significance.

The Old Testament text of Daniel 7:13–14 also aids our understanding of Christ's exaltation:

"One like a Son of Man was coming,
And he came up to the Ancient of Days
And was presented before Him.
"And to Him [the Son of Man] was given dominion,
Glory and a kingdom,
That all the peoples, nations, and men of every language
Might serve Him."

This is prophetic of Jesus' exaltation as the God-man (the Son of man). Jesus picks up on this Daniel passage when he says, "All authority has been given to Me in heaven and on earth" (Matthew 28:18). And this is what Paul means when he writes that after Jesus died on the cross, "God highly exalted Him, and bestowed on Him the name which is above every name" (Philippians 2:9).

Some say that since Jesus was *given* authority, or since he was *given* an exalted status, he therefore did not always have authority or an exalted status. But by saying that, they miss the intent of the Bible. What the Bible is teaching is that by virtue of Christ's humanity, he as perfect man (as well as deity) is now exalted.

Mediator and high priest because of the cross. Always remember that Christ's office as mediator and high priest has its grounding, its foundation, in the cross event. Two Scripture passages in particular show this is so.

In 1 Timothy 2:5, Paul tells Timothy, "For there is one God, and one mediator (Greek *mesitēs*) also between God and men, the man Christ Jesus." From the Greek word *mesitēs* comes the English *meso-*, which is used to denote something that is "in the middle." For example, "Mesopotamia" means "between rivers" (*potamia* is Greek for "rivers"). Our Greek word in 1 Timothy 2:5, then, communicates someone in the middle.

Jesus is our "middle man." He is the one who comes between the Father and us. By virtue of his being God *and* human, Jesus is the perfect one to be our mediator. Now we come to the grounds on which he is so called. Notice the verse immediately following 1 Timothy 2:5: "who gave Himself as a ransom for all" (v. 6). If we take the last part of verse 5 and run it into this verse, we see it more clearly: "There is one mediator also between God and men, the man Christ Jesus, who gave Himself as a ransom." After Paul calls Jesus the one mediator, he quickly cites the fact that Jesus died on the cross (he gave himself as a payment). There can be no doubt that in Paul's thought, Christ's office as mediator is grounded in the cross.

The writer of the book of Hebrews also grounded Christ's mediating role in the cross. In Hebrews 9:14–15 take note of "and for this reason" that begins verse 15 as well as the content of verse 14: "How much more will the blood of Christ, who through the eternal Spirit offered himself without blemish to God, cleanse your conscience from dead works to serve the living God? And for this reason He is the mediator of a new covenant." Do you see the connection? When the writer of Hebrews says, "And for this reason He is the mediator," we look back to verse 14 and see that reason. It is the cross event. Here is another instance of grounding Christ's office of mediator in the cross.

For Discussion

1. What are some further consequences of intently denying Christ's bodily resurrection?

2. Christian **doctrine** is like a garment, for all the threads of doctrine are tied together. How is this the case with Christ's resurrection, ascension, and offices of mediator and high priest?

3. Why do you think the biblical writers grounded Christ's high priesthood and mediatorship in the cross?

4. Christ's resurrection marks his victory over death and thus our eventual victory over death. Discuss some ways in which our conduct in our everyday lives should reflect this truth.

 Meditation

Are We Fans of Jesus Christ?

Thanks be to God, who gives us the victory through our Lord Jesus Christ. (1 Corinthians 15:57)

During a flight home from a conference, I picked up a magazine on the plane. The cover caught my attention and led me to a corresponding article. The picture was of the new home-run king Mark McGwire. He was in the middle of one of his gigantic swings that could drive a ball well beyond 450 feet. His eyes stared directly and intently at the place on the bat upon which the ball would collide, and his huge forearms showed beneath the jersey he wore.

The writer of the article told of how he and his son bonded over McGwire's victory of breaking the single season home-run record of sixty-one by Roger Maris. On the night of McGwire's sixty-second homer, he and his son cheered as if they both were in on it. They shared in the victory. I too was excited. After all, why did the article catch my eye?

I read on. Then a question entered my mind: Do Christians get this excited over Jesus? Do we bond over Jesus' victory over death by his resurrection? As great a feat as was McGwire's, it is obscure in comparison to what Jesus Christ has done. We all need to be reminded, when we cheer for someone's accomplishments, that the greatest hero the universe will ever know is the Lord of glory.

Help me, Lord, to be excited about you. Remind me, Lord, of who you are and what you have done for the salvation of your people. Thank you, Jesus, for your victory over death. In your name. Amen.

PART THREE

Salvation

7

The New Birth, Adoption, and Justification

✚

THE GOSPEL OF JESUS CHRIST IS THE GOOD NEWS OF JESUS Christ. Sharing the gospel means sharing with others that God is holy and just, loving and good, and that we are sinners who have broken God's laws. Consequently we deserve death and eternal punishment, but Jesus has come to offer a sacrifice for sins. He alone is the way of salvation. If we put our trust in him and what he has accomplished, we shall be saved from God's condemnation.

In this chapter we will look into three components of salvation, or the Good News—the new birth, adoption, and justification. In other words, these are the ways in which God saves us. The next chapter will feature three more elements of salvation—sanctification, resurrection, and heaven.

The Basics

Salvation

The wages of sin, Paul says, is death (Romans 6:23). The wages of sin is also eternal condemnation (Matthew 25:41,46). But salvation brings deliverance from these wages (consequences) of sin.

Salvation by grace. There is nothing that we do to merit salvation. It is a gift. Paul tells us, "For by grace you have been saved through faith; and that not of yourselves, it is the gift of God" (Ephesians 2:8). We have been saved by the grace—the unmerited favor—of God. God simply chooses to save us for his glory, and we do nothing to earn that salvation.

Salvation through faith. We are given salvation by God's grace through faith, or trust. God chooses to save us through the vehicle of faith. Ephesians 2:8 explains that even the faith we possess is not of ourselves; it is all of God, lest anyone of us should boast (v. 9).

Jesus as the only way. Jesus says, "I am the way, and the truth, and the life; no one comes to the Father, but through Me" (John 14:6). We live in an age in which this is not a popular message. Because it is not popular, people are more comfortable with multiple ways to heaven. One way, therefore, is just as good as any other. This is what is known as **pluralism** (the ways of salvation are plural, or many) or **inclusivism** (salvation includes all religious paths).

But since Jesus is God's *unique* Son (John 1:14), there can therefore be no other way of salvation. Christianity's message of salvation is therefore *exclusive,* not inclusive.

The place of works. Christianity is also not "easy believe-ism." Paul continues, "For we are His workmanship, created in Christ Jesus for good works, which God prepared beforehand, that we should walk in them" (Ephesians 2:10). True, we have been saved by the grace of God, not by works, but if we are saved, our lives will show it. And lest we think that *we* are doing this of our own power, think again. Paul says that we who are God's work were created in Christ for good works.

The implication of the Good News. Salvation is God's act (one that includes adoption, justification, sanctification, resurrection, and heaven) that saves us from his eternal condemnation. This is "good news" (where the word "gospel" comes from) for humanity. But what makes it "good news"? Must there not be "bad news" that makes this "good news" what it is?

The answer is yes. The bad news is hell. Jesus said that those who do not believe in him will hear these words: "Depart from Me, accursed ones, into the eternal fire which has been prepared for the devil and his angels" (Matthew 25:41). We should parallel that statement with another that occurs just five verses later: "And these will go away into eternal punishment, but the righteous into eternal life" (Matthew 25:46). From these words of our Lord we know that the bad news is likened to existing in eternal fire, which is eternal punishment. This sad and sobering truth is what makes the gospel "good news."

The New Birth

The new birth, or being born again, is what we call "regeneration." To regenerate something is to give it life again. When we are saved, we are given life again. We are born again by the Holy Spirit.

The most popularly cited verse for the new birth is John 3:3, where Jesus tells Nicodemus (a ruler of the Jews), "Unless one is born again, he cannot see the kingdom of God." Jesus then states that being born (generated) in your mother's womb is one thing but being *born again* (regenerated) by the Holy Spirit is another (John 3:5–7). Another phrase also signifies being born again and regeneration—*new creation.* Paul says that "if any man is in Christ [that is, in union with Christ], he is a new creature" (2 Corinthians 5:17).

One more point remains. The phrase "born-again **Christian**" is redundant and serves to cloud the issue by implying that there are other types of Christians. "Born-again Christian" is like "dark black." It is redundant. The only way to be a Christian is to be born again.

Adoption

Adoption is part of our salvation. Because of sin, all humans are estranged from God. Through faith in Christ, we become adopted into a relationship with God. All who believe in Christ become sons and daughters of God by adoption. We then may call God "our Father": "You have received a spirit of adoption as sons by which we cry out, 'Abba! Father!'" (Romans 8:15).

Justification

Justification is also part of our salvation. Paul says we are "justified by faith" (Romans 5:1). When we have trust (faith) in Christ, the Father then declares that we are righteous (just) in his sight. The Father once for all declares that we have been "acquitted," set free from the penalty of eternal condemnation. *Justification*, then, is a declaration by God that we are just in the Deity's sight.

But it is not that we are simply *declared* righteous. No, by faith in Christ we *have* the "righteousness of God" (not our own righteousness) declared upon us by God (Romans 3:22). Christ's righteousness is declared on the believer because Christ did it all, living a righteous life by keeping the whole law of God on our behalf.

For Discussion

1. What is salvation?

2. Is salvation the free gift of God to us? Think of an everyday illustration that would teach this.

3. What are the three components of salvation that are listed in this chapter?

4. Use the words "regeneration," "adoption," and "justification" in a statement of faith. Take a moment to write it.

Beyond the Basics

Prior to Regeneration

Paul's words in Romans 8:29–30 lead us to suspect that there is more going on in the perfect plan of God than we have discussed. Is there anything prior to regeneration (being born again)? The answer certainly appears to be yes. Paul writes, "For whom He [God] foreknew, He also predestined to become conformed to the image of His Son . . . and whom He predestined, these He also called; and whom He called, these He also justified" (Romans 8:29–30). The words in this passage that need clarification are "foreknew," "predestined," and "called."

Foreknew. Christians are not of one mind regarding the subject of God's foreknowledge. Still it is essential that we explore this aspect of **theology.**

Those who are to become saved are said to be "foreknown" by God. The word "know," when in the context of the relationship between God and God's people—and this is certainly the context here—means "having an intimate relationship with God" (see Jeremiah 1:5; Amos 3:2; Hosea 13:5; 1 Corinthians 8:3; Galatians 4:8). It connotes a closeness of association, a deep affection. With "fore" preceding the word "know," it simply means "to know intimately beforehand." The word is applied to those whom God set his love upon from all eternity (before they ever came into existence). The meaning, then, is that God "foreloved" us. Thus, God's choosing of Christians for salvation is absolutely unconditional (see Romans 9:11–13).

Some Christians disagree with this meaning of "foreknow." Rather than seeing it as "foreloved," they view it as God's "knowing beforehand" who would believe in him. These, they say, are those whom God saves. The difference may seem elementary at first, and indeed there are even variations on these two views, but this is an "in-house" debate you will surely enter into with Christians in the future.

Predestined. Those who are to become saved are "predestined." In other words, God determines that those whom he foreknew will be saved (conformed to the image of God's Son; that is, restored to the original "image of God" enjoyed by Adam before the Fall; see Genesis 1:26–2:25). God determines this beforehand.

Called. Whereas being "foreknown"and "predestined" refers to the time *before* our existence, being "called" refers to the time *of* our existence. Paul says that those whom God predestines for salvation are "called."

It is God who foreknows, it is God who predestines, and it is God who calls. We can say that this word means "draws." God draws us to himself in different ways. God's calling of one person is most likely different from God's calling of another. Some of us experience the "lightning bolt" calling, while others have been raised in the Christian faith and cannot pinpoint the exact time and place of God's calling.

The Gospel of Matthew casts another light on the subject of being called. Matthew 22:14 states, "Many are called, but few are chosen." What does this mean? In preaching the gospel, millions of Christians have extended the invitation to others to come to Christ. In this sense there is a universal call, but note that "few are chosen." The Gospel thus points to a *general* calling, whereas Paul refers to God's *special* calling of the ones foreknown and predestined.

Romans 8:30 teaches that those whom God has called, "He also justified." This translation doesn't quite capture the nuance of the Greek verb *dikaioō*, which means "to pronounce as justified." In other words, God *declares* (pronounces) us as just (righteous, acquitted) in his sight.

Note that each of these aspects of salvation—being foreknown, predestined, called, and justified—is all about God. God is the one who foreknows, who predestines, who calls, and who pronounces justification.

Adoption and Redemption

Salvation includes adoption, for Christians are said to be adopted children. Now there is a sense in which all people are God's children *by creation;* however, not all are God's children *by salvation.* This is the adoptive sense. Some think that only the first category exists and that all will be saved. They fail to see that the Bible speaks of the second category as well and that this second category alone pertains to salvation.

In Romans 8 Paul refers to "adoption." After stating that Christians "have received a spirit of adoption as sons" (8:15), he states in verse 16 that "the Spirit Himself bears witness with our spirit that we are children of God." Thus, "adoption as sons" (v. 15) leads to being counted as "children of God" (v. 16).

Adoption by redemption. The Bible says that in the fullness of time, "God sent forth His Son, born of a woman, born under the Law, in order that He might redeem those who were under the Law, that we might receive the adoption as sons" (Galatians 4:4–5). Paul's sequencing here teaches us that redeeming brings about adoption. But what does it mean to *redeem?* The basic meaning is "to buy it." **Redemption** therefore is "the act of buying something back."

Kinsman redeemer. No discussion of redemption is complete without the Old Testament motif of "kinsman redeemer." Though this seems strange to many of our culture, it was not strange in the ancient culture of the Israelites.

A certain law (known as the "levirate law") stated that if a woman's husband died and left her childless, the next of kin was to step in and marry the woman. If she then birthed a son, that firstborn son would be considered the son of the deceased. This kinsman who stepped in for the deceased is the "redeemer." The Hebrew word for redeemer is *gō'ēl* (one who buys back).

The role of the kinsman redeemer was crucial in ancient Israel because a woman who was childless and without a husband was outright destitute. When the kinsman redeemer stepped in and "bought" the woman, he was bringing her into (or keeping her within) the family compound, thus giving her a place in the family.

In the Old Testament story of Ruth is a wonderful example of the *gō'ēl*. Naomi, Ruth's mother-in-law, lost both her husband and her two sons. One of the deceased sons was married to Ruth. Naomi and Ruth were now widows, and Ruth had no children by her husband. Enter Boaz. Boaz (after the first in line to redeem declined) was the *gō'ēl* of Naomi and Ruth. Boaz marries Ruth (Naomi was beyond childbearing years) and takes both Naomi and Ruth into his family compound.

Elsewhere in the Old Testament God is called Israel's Redeemer (Psalm 78:35). Given the cultural background, the term is pregnant with meaning. God is the one who bought back the people, rescuing them from slavery and making them God's own people. God is the *gō'ēl*.

Have you ever wondered what Jesus meant by the words, "In my Father's house are many dwelling places . . . I go to prepare a place for you" (John 14:2)? Jesus is saying that he is our *gō'ēl*, our kinsman redeemer! The Old Testament picture of Naomi and Ruth being redeemed by Boaz is carried into the New Testament with Christ as our Redeemer. Christ has "bought us back," redeemed us, and is preparing a place for us in his Father's family compound—heaven.

Recalling Paul's teaching in Galatians 4:4–5, we gather that Christ's redemption of us brings about our adoption as children of God. But that redemption was costly. In the words of Paul, "You have been bought with a price" (1 Corinthians 6:20). That price was the precious blood of Christ, our Redeemer. As Paul writes elsewhere, "In Him we have redemption through His blood" (Ephesians 1:7).

The Place of Works in Salvation

How should we view good works (obedience)? A healthy view of the place of works in the Christian life starts with God. Indeed, when we Christians recognize the components of the **covenant** between us and God, it forever changes the way in which we view obedience. The covenant formula, or wording, is simple yet profound: We "do" because God "did."

The Old Testament. The Old Testament teaches us what is contained in the covenant (agreement) between God and God's people. Many ingredients make up a covenant: stipulations, oaths, blessings, and curses—but a covenant starts with what we call the "historical prologue." The historical prologue of Deuteronomy 5:6 occurs just before the Ten Commandments: "I am the LORD your God, who brought you out of the land of Egypt."

Remember that how we view obedience starts with God. And note that the historical prologue of Deuteronomy 5:6 is immediately followed by the Ten Commandments. In other words, the things we ought not do and the things we are to do (the Ten Commandments) are based upon who God is and what God has done ("I am the LORD your God who brought you out of the land of Egypt"). We "do" *because* God "did."

The New Testament. With the New Testament comes a new covenant between God and humanity, but similarities between it and the ones in the Old Testament are clear. Our obedience to God's commands continues as an essential element of the agreement.

Matthew 28 begins with the resurrection of Jesus (vv. 1–15). In verse 16 we read that Jesus appeared on a mountain. Note the parallel to Mount Sinai, where the LORD appeared for the giving of the law. In the ancient Near East the Deity commonly appeared on a mountain, which is why "they worshiped Him" (28:17). Jesus then says, "All authority has been given to Me in heaven and on earth" (v. 18). Then, as when the LORD gave the law to Moses, Jesus gives the Eleven his commandments: "Go therefore and make disciples of all the nations, baptizing them . . . teaching them . . ." (vv. 19–20). Do you see what is going on? The commandments in verses 19–20 are based upon who Jesus is and what he has done (vv. 16–18).

Philippians 3:20–21 tells us who Jesus is and what he *will* do: "The Lord Jesus Christ, who will transform the body of our humble state into conformity with the body of His glory." And, of course, in the very next verse (4:1), which begins with "therefore," Paul exhorts Christians to "stand firm." Several more exhortations follow. Once again, what we are to do is based upon who God is and what God has done (or will do).

Another example occurs in 1 Corinthians 6:20. Note that after Paul says, "You have been bought with a price," he immediately follows with, "therefore glorify God in your body." Our obedience to God's commands is based upon God's action. In other words, we do *because* God did.

Christians must never forget that it was the LORD who delivered them "out of the land of Egypt." Because God rescued us by grace, we must be obedient. As Paul says, we are called to "obedience that comes from faith" (Romans 1:5, NIV).

For Discussion

1. God foreknows, predestines, and calls those to be justified. Discuss how this gives the Christian peace in her or his life.

2. Discuss the meaning of "redeemer" in the Old Testament and how Christ has fulfilled this Old Testament type. What, then, is the meaning of Christ's pronouncement, "In My Father's house are many dwelling places"?

3. The Christian view of works must start with who God is and what God has done. In other words, we "do" *because* God "did." Discuss the Christian view of the relationship between salvation and works. Give an everyday illustration of this teaching.

 **Meditation**

Justification

Being justified as a gift by his grace through the redemption which is in Christ Jesus. (Romans 3:24)

I recall an episode of *Star Trek: The Next Generation*. In it some aliens called the humans of the *Starship Enterprise* "ugly bags of mostly water." It was an amusing and humorous description that made me begin to think. Though the aliens' use of the phrase had no spiritual connotations, it would do us well to place it in that context for a moment.

Think of all that we and the rest of humanity have done in our lives that breaks God's laws. Further, think of it collectively, if indeed you are able, over thousands and thousands of years! It is an "ugly" picture. We have stolen, lied, cheated, committed adultery and murder (if not physically, surely with our hearts), hated, despised, and the list goes on.

We must come under the judgment of God. We must! Yet, God graciously has planned to save some from among these "ugly bags." The almighty God determined to give us new birth, adopt us, make us children of God, and justify us in Christ. The Deity would do it by sending his very own Son to take upon himself the punishment due to us. As a result, we who trust in the Father's Son are "justified" (acquitted) by the Father. We are—and let us never use the term lightly—forgiven.

Your grace is amazing, O God. I praise you, Lord, and I will meditate upon this, and be thankful.

8

Sanctification, Resurrection, and Heaven

✠

WE ARE ABOUT TO CONSIDER THE FINAL DESTINATION THAT IS included in the salvation of God's people—heaven. But before we do that, we need to explore the last two of the five steps that lead to heaven in all its fullness—sanctification and resurrection.

The Basics

Sanctification

Sanctification continues what the new birth, adoption, and justification began. There are two basic aspects of the process of sanctification.

First and foremost, sanctification is the ongoing process of making us more and more holy. Right now we are undergoing a process of moral change through the Holy Spirit's ministry of sanctification (see 1 Peter 1:2). Though not yet fully complete, it will be one day (remember that justification is God's once-for-all declaration that we are righteous in his sight, while sanctification is an ongoing process).

The purpose of sanctification is that we may be able to dwell with the Lord forever in heaven. God will not put up with

77

imperfection forever. There will come a time when only righteous and perfect creatures in Christ are permitted to dwell with
God and be God's people. Sanctification brings us to that end.

Second, sanctification is the ongoing process of setting the
Christian apart for service to God. The Holy Spirit indwells
believers and empowers them for individual ministry to the
world and to God's people. In other words, God saves you and
then, by the Holy Spirit, uses you to accomplish the divine will.
This is a privilege we do not deserve. It happens only by God's
grace. Because it is a privilege (after all, it is not as if God really
needs us!) and comes as a free gift, we ought to find joy in our
sanctification.

Resurrection

Resurrection begins the study of **eschatology.** The Lord's act of
raising us from the dead (or if he comes back while we are yet
living, changing us in a microsecond) is called "resurrection."
Put simply, Christ is going to give us bodies that are without
corruption, decay, and sin. In the great resurrection chapter
known as 1 Corinthians 15, Paul comforts us with these words:
"We shall all be changed, in a moment, in the twinkling of an
eye . . . the dead will be raised imperishable" (vv. 51–52).

Resurrection is also **glorification.** Paul says that all those
whom God justifies will also be glorified (Romans 8:30). This is
glory, not in the sense that we are God ourselves, but in the
sense that our moral nature and our bodies are perfected, allow-
ing us to live forever. In a sense, glorification is the end of the
sanctification process.

Jesus in his now glorified humanity is the great type of what we
will become at the resurrection. Philippians 3:21 informs us that
our present bodies will be conformed to his glorious body. Whatever this means in all its fullness, we will not know until we get
there, but at least it means that whatever Jesus now is in his glorified humanity, we will be. This is what John means when he says,
"Beloved, now we are children of God, and it has not appeared as
yet what we shall be. We know that, when He appears, we shall be
like Him, because we shall see Him just as He is" (1 John 3:2).

Heaven

In the Bible are at least two meanings of the word "heaven." First, *heaven* is that which refers to the universe. It is used this way in Genesis 1:1: "In the beginning God created the heavens and the earth." Our focus is on the second meaning of heaven as "the place of God." It is used in this way by Jesus, who teaches us to pray to "our Father who art in heaven" (Matthew 6:9). Further, Christ ascended to the Father who is in heaven and also continually exercises his office as mediator in heaven: "For Christ did not enter a holy place made with hands, a mere copy of the true one, but into heaven itself, now to appear in the presence of God for us" (Hebrews 9:24).

What heaven will be. Right now heaven is beyond our physical perception, but the Bible gives us some idea of what heaven will be. Christian eschatology, for instance, talks of heaven as Eden restored, a place where the present heaven of God will become united with the things on earth. Heaven is, as Paul writes, "the summing up of all things in Christ, things in the heavens and things upon the earth" (Ephesians 1:10). The realities of the new heaven and earth as listed in Revelation 21–22 strongly suggest a restoring of what was lost in the garden of Eden. Both humanity (those righteous in Christ) *and* the creation are restored to the original perfection talked about in Genesis 1–2.

For example, Revelation 21:4 tells us that "there shall no longer be any death . . . or pain." This is the reversing of the curses listed in Genesis 3. By disobeying the LORD, Adam and Eve brought death upon themselves (and us). God said that if they disobeyed, they would "surely die" (Genesis 2:17). After Adam and Eve's sin, death became a reality, for God then said, "To dust you shall return" (Genesis 3:19). As for pain, a specific curse is pronounced upon Eve: "In pain you shall bring forth children" (Genesis 3:16).

One final example, which does not exhaust the list, is found in Revelation 22:2. Describing the New Jerusalem, John says, "And on either side of the river was the tree of life." This "tree of life" does sound familiar! It is found in Genesis 2:9: "The tree of life [was] also in the midst of the garden." Heaven is going to be "paradise on earth." We will indeed live forever in heaven.

I saved the most important characteristic of heaven for last: heaven is the place of the presence of God. What is the goal of all this? God is. Whom are we to desire? We are to desire God. Heaven is the fullness of the **reconciliation** of humanity to God, which was already begun in Christ. Heaven is living forever in glorified bodies in the awesome presence of the God of the universe.

For Discussion

1. What are the two aspects of sanctification?

2. Resurrection is God's raising us from the dead, giving us new glorified bodies. What does this enable us to do in the future?

3. Heaven is described in the book of Revelation as Eden restored. Take time to discuss how God has been preparing us to be in the divine presence in the new Eden.

Beyond the Basics

Sanctification

The Greek word for "sanctification" is *hagiasmos,* which has the two basic meanings of (1) a change in one's moral condition and (2) being set apart. Both these senses of sanctification are used together in exhortation to us.

We are called to be *set apart morally* for service to God. Though we rest on the great truth that it is God who is acting for our sanctification, there must be evidence of this in our lives. Paul exhorts Christians to "glorify God in [or with] your body" (1 Corinthians 6:20). In another place, Paul states, "I urge you therefore, brethren, by the mercies of God, to present your bodies as a living and holy sacrifice, acceptable to God" (Romans 12:1).

God chooses all believers and sets them apart for salvation. Peter says that we are "A CHOSEN RACE, A royal PRIESTHOOD, A HOLY [set apart] NATION, A PEOPLE FOR God's OWN POSSESSION, that . . . [we] may proclaim the excellencies of Him" (1 Peter 2:9).

We, therefore, are set apart by God to proclaim the divine excellencies and to glorify him.

Are we saints? If you are a Christian, you are at present a saint! The Greek word for "sanctification" *(hagiasmos)* comes from the Greek word for "saint" *(hagios).* Recognizing the similarity between the words helps us understand our own sainthood as well as Paul's words to the Christians at Ephesus: "Paul, an apostle of Christ Jesus by the will of God, to the saints who are at Ephesus" (Ephesians 1:1). Whether in Paul's time or our own, anyone who is a Christian is a saint, a *sanctified* (holy) one.

A crucial aspect of sanctification. In order that believers might live forever in the presence of God in heaven, we must be "conformed to the image of His [God's] Son" (Romans 8:29). Paul's words point to a crucial aspect of sanctification. Note the apostle's use of the word "image," which is a loaded theological term that contains many shades of meaning. One in particular is applicable to our study. When Paul uses "image," we are reminded of the original "image" of God mentioned in Genesis 1:26–27. When God created Adam "in His own image," "image" meant nothing short of perfection. Recall that "God saw all that He had made, and behold, it was very good" (Genesis 1:31).

God is bringing us to the point at which the original perfect "image" of Adam in the garden of Eden is fully restored. Through the process of sanctification, God makes us fit for the new heaven and the new earth (Eden once again!). But in order to get to that place, sanctification must lead to our being "changed, in a moment, in the twinkling of an eye" (1 Corinthians 15:51–52). This is the resurrection.

The Resurrection

All will rise, indeed, but not all will rise to eternal life. Some will rise to judgment. The New Testament **doctrine** of the resurrection, which includes these two different destinations for the resurrected, is grounded in the Old Testament. The dead "shall come forth," says Jesus, "those who did the good deeds to a resurrection of life, those who committed the evil deeds to a resurrection of judgment" (John 5:29). Jesus was alluding to the prophet Daniel: "Many of those who sleep in the dust of the ground will awake, these to everlasting life, but the others to disgrace and everlasting contempt" (Daniel 12:2).

Resurrection to life. God promises to raise his people from the dead. The prophet Ezekiel was commanded to prophesy to God's people, saying, "Thus says the Lord GOD, 'Behold, I will open your graves and cause you to come up out of your graves, My people'" (Ezekiel 37:12; see also v. 13). In 1 Corinthians 15 Paul says, "We shall all be changed . . . in the twinkling of an eye" and "will be raised imperishable" (vv. 51–52). The "we" are the **covenant** people of God. "We" are God's people.

Those who rise to a resurrection of life are those who have died believing in the biblical Christ. Paul calls the resurrection "the victory" (1 Corinthians 15:57). The victory is that death has been defeated by the resurrection of Christ and will be fully realized in us when we are raised from the dead to live forever in the presence of God.

Resurrected to judgment. Every person—all those who have come before us, those we meet in our daily lives, and those still to be born—is either going to be resurrected to eternal life or to eternal judgment. It is a sobering thought.

Those who in this life do not accept Jesus Christ as their Lord and Savior will be resurrected to judgment. As witnessed above, the prophet Daniel noted that some would be raised to "everlasting contempt." Jesus talks about this in relation to "the day of judgment." The nature of this judgment is the opposite of the eternal life that the righteous in Christ will receive. In Matthew 25:41 and 25:46, Jesus describes this judgment as "eternal fire" and "eternal punishment."

The book of Revelation describes this eternal fire and eternal punishment as "the lake of fire," the place into which the beast and the false prophet are thrown. And there the two "will be tormented day and night forever and ever" (Revelation 20:10). Sadly, those who are not in Christ and whose names are "not found written in the book of life" will be "thrown into the lake of fire" (Revelation 20:15) and will suffer the punishment of torment forever.

The hour of the resurrection. When will the resurrection to life or to judgment take place? This is a good question to ask, but don't expect an easy answer. You can be confident of two points, however. First, though Christians should never claim to know the exact time of Christ's coming, there are certain events mentioned in the Bible for which we are to watch. Second, even though Christians will disagree with some of the particulars of one another's answer, they agree on one very important part of the response—they all believe *that* Jesus is coming back. In other words, all Christians agree on Christ's "second coming," after which they will dwell in God's presence forever.

Despite the general agreement on the reality of Christ's second coming, Christians hold differing views of end-time persecution and the millennium. Such matters relate to the specific branch of **theology** known as eschatology. The labels used to identify the three basic views of the time of persecution known as the **great tribulation** are **pretribulationism, midtribulationism,** and **posttribulationism.** Three basic positions have arisen on the millennium as well—**premillennialism, amillennialism,** and **postmillennialism.** Christians may disagree in these views, but again, they all believe that Christ is coming back.

Heaven

After Christ's second coming, Christians will be resurrected and will live forever in the presence of God in heaven. According to Revelation 21–22, the new heaven and the new earth is the garden of Eden restored. There the resurrected righteous in Christ will dwell forever in the presence of God. Biblical parallels between John's description of the new heaven and new earth (in the book of Revelation) and the garden of Eden (in Genesis) help us understand more about the future destination of God's people.

Intimacy with God. Genesis 3:8 implies that the relationship between God and Adam and Eve was of the highest intimacy. Adam and Eve "heard the sound of the LORD God walking in the garden," which shows that they once enjoyed his direct presence. In Genesis 3:24 the LORD "drove the man out" of the garden of Eden after he sinned (we should assume that Eve was driven out with him). The significance of this driving out is that Adam and Eve were no longer in the presence of God. The relationship between the Creator and the created is restored in Revelation 21:3: "And I heard a loud voice from the throne, saying, 'Behold, the tabernacle of God is among men, and He shall dwell among them, and they shall be His people, and God Himself shall be among them.'"

Access to the water of life. The unmistakable parallel between Genesis 2:10 and Revelation 22:1 provides more evidence that heaven is Eden restored. Genesis 2:10 reads, "Now a river flowed out of Eden." Revelation 22:1 speaks of the new heaven and new earth having "a river of the water of life, clear as crystal, coming from the throne of God and of the Lamb." Also note that just after Eden's river is mentioned in Genesis 2:10, one of the rivers (the Pishon) flowing out from that main river is associated with gold, bdellium, and onyx (vv. 11–12). Revelation 21:18–21 features all the precious elements that are associated with the river of the water of life. This water of life signifies God as the source of our salvation; the river's presence in the new heaven and earth signifies God's presence with us there forever.

Impure no more. The sin of Adam and Eve in the garden of Eden was of such magnitude that they became sinful creatures. Since nothing impure could stay in God's presence in the garden, the Lord drove them out (Genesis 3:24). Anything impure was outside, which has been the dwelling place of God's people ever since.

In the book of Revelation, the New Eden is no different from the original in that anything to do with sin is not allowed inside: "Outside are the dogs and the sorcerers and the immoral persons and the murderers and the idolaters, and everyone who loves and practices lying" (Revelation 22:15). However, the dwelling place of God's people will change. Once purified, they will reside in, not outside, the New Eden.

The promise of heaven. What a great promise God has given! I pray that our desire will always be God. I pray that our desire will always be to see God's glory. Wanting heaven *is* wanting

God. Rejoice and stand on this promise: "He who overcomes shall inherit these things, and I will be his God and he will be My son" (Revelation 21:7).

For Discussion

1. An important purpose of sanctification is becoming "conformed to the image" of Christ. Is this "image" what Adam was before the Fall?

2. Being conformed to Christ's image allows us to dwell in God's presence forever in the new heaven and new earth (Eden restored). Why do you think this "conforming" is important?

3. All people will be resurrected—some to eternal life, some to eternal judgment. Discuss how this might bring a new perspective on how we view others.

4. Fill in the blank: Desiring heaven is desiring _____.

✛ Meditation

Antz's Best Is Our Worst; Our Best Is God's Best

And [He] showed me the holy city, Jerusalem, coming down out of heaven from God. (Revelation 21:10)

Watching the movie *Antz* does something to the viewer's perspective. The animated movie is set among a colony of ants, and it gives humans a glimpse of our world from the ants' perspective. Up close the antz's colony seemed oh so big. But when the camera rose up high, their world was shown to be really quite small.

Among the antz there was talk about utopia—a place that was beyond any pleasures they could imagine. They called it "insectopia." Some believed; some doubted. The hero ant was bent on finding this place, this ultimate paradise.

When he got there, it was all he was led to believe it was— and more! Empty soft-drink cans, half-eaten and rotting sandwiches there for the taking, and other assorted "goodies" thrilled the ant. Then the camera began to rise, revealing to us that this was the garbage of a small segment of a park outside a city! Truly the antz's best was our worst.

Such is not so with God. God's best is our best because God's own self is our utopia. God's heaven is our heaven. God foreknew us, predestined us, called us, justified us, and will glorify us. God has begun to fit us for the Jerusalem to come. Rejoice.

Our Father, we praise you. We praise you above all. Give us desire for you. Make us long to be in your presence in your heaven forever. Thank you that your best is our best. By your grace and in the name of your Son. Amen.

PART FOUR

Therefore . . .

9

The Christian Life and the Church

✠

THE PRECEDING CHAPTERS HAVE EXPLORED WHO GOD IS AND what God has done. It is fitting then that this concluding chapter turns to our response to God's mighty acts—our response as individuals as we live **Christian** lives and our collective response as the Church. This chapter is the only one in the book that does not include a "Basics" section and a "Beyond the Basics" section. Why? Because it simply does not seem right to think of a *"basic* Christian life" and a *"beyond-the-basic* Christian life," does it? Let's begin.

The Christian Life

In a certain yet vital sense, the life of the Christian is a way of witness to family, friends, and others that one has been saved by the grace of God. The Christian life then is the evidence of salvation because it is one big "therefore." What this means is really quite simple and can be explained by the statement, "The indicative precedes the imperative." In other words, because of who God is and what God has done (the indicative—a stated fact), we *therefore* live according to God's rules (the imperative—

commands that follow). In the Bible are many examples of the indicative preceding the imperative. We'll focus on two—one from the Old Testament and one from the New Testament.

The Ten Commandments listed in Exodus 20:3–17 (and in Deuteronomy 5:7–21) are preceded by a statement from the LORD: "I am the LORD your God, who brought you out of the land of Egypt" (Exodus 20:2; Deuteronomy 5:6). Remember that the indicative concerns who God is and what God has done. In this case the indicative is very straightforward: God is God and has saved his people. After this, the imperatives—the Ten Commandments—follow. The life of believers in the one true God is one big "therefore." Take a moment now to read Exodus 20:1–17, keeping in mind the formula that the indicative precedes the imperative.

In the New Testament, the apostle Paul writes, "When Christ, who is our life, is revealed, then you also will be revealed with Him in glory. Therefore consider the members of your earthly body as dead to immorality, impurity, passion, evil desire, and greed, which amounts to idolatry" (Colossians 3:4–5). Here the indicative is that Christ is going to come back again to judge the world and that those who believe in Christ will be glorified and live forever with him. Paul then follows with the imperative, and the word "therefore" in the verse signals it. In other words, Paul is saying that because of who Christ is and what he is going to do, we ought to live a certain way.

How Should We Live?

Since all **theology** starts with God, let's explore how we should live by starting with God, paying careful attention to the italicized words: *Since* God is God and has brought about not only our physical existence but our eternal life as well, *therefore* we ought to live for God by faith. This implies two things that should not be separated: (1) living to glorify God *by* (2) obeying God's commands. Paul, under the inspiration of God the Holy Spirit, sums it up beautifully. With the indicative preceding the imperative, he says, "You have been bought with a price: therefore glorify God in your body" (1 Corinthians 6:20).

Obviously it is beyond the scope of a relatively short book such as this to list all facets of the Christian life. But I shall mention several that seem essential and that should start the ball rolling.

Therefore preach the gospel to others. Jesus commands us: "Go therefore and make disciples of all the nations, baptizing them in the name of the Father and the Son and the Holy Spirit" (Matthew 28:19; see also what precedes this command in v. 18!).

The Christian life should thus be characterized by a willingness to seize upon every open door to share the gospel with others (see Colossians 4:3). The word "gospel" means "good news." The Good News is that even though people are sinners and deserve God's judgment of eternal punishment, God in the **person** of Jesus has come to give his life as a sacrifice for sin so that all who call upon Jesus (trust in him as Lord and Savior) will be saved (see 1 Corinthians 15:1–4; Romans 3:23; 6:23; 10:9,13).

Therefore baptize and teach others. In the second half of Matthew 28:19, Jesus states that disciples (Christians) are to be baptized. In turn they are to baptize others. There are different ways of conducting water baptism among Christians. Some sprinkle water on the believer, some pour, and some fully immerse believers into water.

Notwithstanding these differences in practice, the point is to be obedient to Christ and be baptized. Please note that Christians are saved by grace through faith and not by works (Ephesians 2:8–9). Baptism, then, is an act of obedience that is *characteristic* of a Christian, as is the next act that Jesus commands.

Jesus continues in Matthew 28:20: "Teaching them to observe all that I commanded you." Another characteristic of disciples then is obedience as demonstrated in the teaching of others. Believers are to pass on the torch, so to speak.

Therefore live in peace, joy, and fear. Jesus said, "Peace I leave with you; My peace I give to you; not as the world gives, do I give to you. Let not your heart be troubled, nor let it be fearful" (John 14:27). Generally, peace, understood as tranquility and calmness, should characterize the Christian life.

I believe the main reason for peace in the Christian life is found in Romans 8:28–30. But let's start with verse 31 and work backward. Why does Paul ask, "If God is for us, who can be against us?" (NIV)? His question implies the answer, "No one." What he means is that when all things are said and done, since God foreknew us, predestined us, called us, justified us, and will glorify us (vv. 29–30), God will work out all things together for good (v. 28). This does not mean that Christians will be exempt from pain and suffering. For example, believers are not free from contracting diseases that will take their earthly lives. We all experience tragedies. Rather, it means that in the midst of all these, we are to remember the big picture—God's salvation. *Therefore,* in the midst of suffering and death, we are to have peace (see Philippians 4:6–7).

As for joy, there is no better reason for joy than recognizing who God is and what God has done. A seminary professor once instructed me concerning Psalm 118:24: "This is the day which the LORD has made." "Rather than 'has *made,*'" he said, "'has *acted*' is more accurate." The psalm exhorts us to rejoice during this day. We should *therefore* rejoice because of who God is and because God has acted for the salvation of his people. Indeed, this is the day that the LORD has acted!

Are we therefore to go around, no matter what, with smiles on our faces twenty-four hours a day? Obviously not, for even Jesus did not do that. As John tells us, Jesus wept at the sight of the dead Lazarus (John 11:35). Though there will be times of sadness, joy (like peace) is something that should generally characterize the Christian life.

Remember too that Jesus' weeping is not the end of the Lazarus story. Jesus, moments later, raised him from the dead. By doing this, Jesus was pointing to at least two things. First, he was demonstrating to us that one day there will be a resurrection and that he has the power to raise the dead. Second, Jesus was demonstrating to us that Satan and his power over death had been defeated (see Hebrews 2:14–17). The result of all this in our lives—the *therefore*—is that we should rejoice because the devil has been rendered ultimately powerless.

At this point you might be asking, "How can I have joy, peace, and *fear* at the same time?" You can if by fear you mean "awe, reverence, and respect." This fear—awe, reverence, respect—should characterize our lives and be directed to God because of who God is and what God has done. The Bible says, "The fear of the Lord is the beginning of knowledge" (Proverbs 1:7). In other words, wisdom comes from a healthy respect for God.

Yet even within this definition of fear as awe, reverence, and respect, there arises a sense of "being afraid." I think this is healthy. Being afraid of God is healthy if it is put in its proper context. If we revere, are in awe of, and respect God, we will also (again in a healthy sense) be afraid of God. Likewise in a healthy family relationship between parents and a child, the child should admire the parents but also fear their discipline. This contributes to healthy nurturing. So, put in this proper context, we are to fear God and strive to do what God commands because God and God alone is perfectly and infinitely holy.

The apostle Peter explains that "the day of the Lord" is coming, during which the great judgment will occur when "the earth and all its works will be burned up" (2 Peter 3:10). Peter then asks the proper question, "Since all these things are to be destroyed in this way, what sort of people ought you to be [?]" (v. 11). Peter then states that we are to be diligent and found "in peace, spotless and blameless" (v. 14).

Can We Be Perfect?

No, we can't be perfect (though one day we will—at the resurrection). We must, however, strive by the grace of God through the ministry of the Holy Spirit to be perfect, for Jesus commands us to do this (Matthew 5:48). And for this reason we must not take our salvation as a license to sin (see Romans 6:1–2). The Christian life should be one characterized by the desire to be perfect and the striving to be perfect.

Enter sin. Sin and its consequences are terrible realities, and that is what makes the Good News (the gospel) so great for the unbeliever. Sin is also a terrible reality for the Christian because it is inevitable that we all will sin. Yet, the blood of Jesus Christ is also great news for the Christian.

The apostle John defines sin as "lawlessness" (1 John 1:4). Thus, sin is breaking the laws of God. We have all done it. We will all do it. Miraculously, Christ is the remedy. The marvelous news is that Christ's blood and its cleansing power continue throughout the Christian's life. This could be called the gospel for Christians! In 1 John 1:7 John says, "The blood of Jesus . . . cleanses us from all sin." "Cleanses" is in the present tense. In other words, Jesus' blood *keeps on* cleansing us from all sin. Confession, though, is important. In verse 9 John writes, "If we confess our sins, He is faithful and righteous to forgive us our sins." Yes, we will indeed fail God many times, but if we confess our sins, God will keep on forgiving us.

The irony. Many Christians wonder if they are still Christians because of sin in their lives. There is a great irony to this, for if they weren't Christians in the first place, they would not be wondering whether or not they are Christians! That is, if the Holy Spirit didn't convict them, they would not even entertain the question. The fact is, the Holy Spirit's ministry is to convict us when we sin, and this leads to confession to the Father to have mercy upon us and forgive us through Christ.

Summary

The true Christian is one who acknowledges who God truly is and what God has done. The true Christian's life is one big "therefore." The true Christian *therefore* lives by faith and strives by God's grace to live according to God's will. Peace and joy and a healthy fear of God *therefore* will also characterize the true Christian's life. The true Christian, though failing miserably, will *therefore* always be convicted of that failure and be moved to the Father by the Holy Spirit to confess sin. The true Christian is *therefore* always continually forgiven through Christ's blood. And, through the miracle and wonder of God's grace, the true Christian is *therefore* always used of God.

For Discussion

1. Why is the Christian life one big "therefore"?

2. What does the Christian life evidence?

3. How do we glorify God?

4. In the example of 2 Peter 3:10 and following, can you explain how the indicative precedes the imperative?

5. Find an example of the indicative and imperative in the Bible other than those mentioned in this and other chapters. How is this passage calling you to live?

The Church

God works through the Church. For this reason we ought to explore, even if briefly, what the meaning of "church" is and its role in our lives.

The first and primary meaning of "church" refers to all Christians throughout the world whom God has called to be his people. The Greek word *ekklēsia* refers to those who have been "called out" of the world to be God's people. Collectively those people are known as "the Church." A secondary meaning of "church" refers to individual and smaller collections of God's people within the Church. These are local churches (in the lowercase). This is the meaning we have in mind when we say, "I am going to church."

It is within churches (in part) that God blesses the Church. The individual church functions within God's Church, and we must not forget the larger and primary meaning (Church) when discussing the individual church to which we belong. The role of the local church, then, will close our chapter.

Why Go?

Hebrews 10:21,25 answers the question regarding the reason why Christians should go to church. And, no surprise by now, the indicative precedes the imperative: "Since we have a great priest over the house of God [the Church; i.e., all believers] . . . [let us not forsake] our own assembling together." Because of who Christ is, God's people are to come together on a continual basis.

Functions of the Church

Churches fulfill many roles. Though all of them cannot be cited here, some very important roles must be mentioned.

Christians go to church to worship God with joyful hearts. Worship is giving expression to the "worth" of God (*worth*ship). Therefore, we worship God because of who God is and what God has done. Worship itself takes many forms—praying, singing, keeping company with other Christians, and study, for instance. We are told in Acts 2 that baptized believers continually devoted themselves "to the apostles' teaching and to fellowship, and to the breaking of bread and to prayer" (v. 42). The local church is God's way of maturing and encouraging Christians (his Church).

Another purpose of churches relates to the preaching of the gospel. As part of the Church, each of us is called to preach the gospel to others. But individual churches should also preach the gospel through their various meetings and outreach ministries.

Yet another role of churches involves various social concerns. Of top priority is to care for the needy and those who are suffering. James is clear as to the definition of true religion: "This is pure and undefiled religion in the sight of our God and Father, to visit orphans and widows in their distress, and to keep oneself unstained by the world" (James 1:27). A second social concern is speaking out against injustice and unrighteousness. John the Baptist did this, though it cost him his life, and Jesus did it as well. Christians, then, should be God's voice to the world regarding such sins as abortion, stealing, adultery, etc., while at the same time emphasizing that all are in need of Christ's saving power and grace.

Further, churches should be involved in disciplining those who have sinned. Unfortunately, most Christians cringe at the thought. Thinking it is not loving to discipline someone, by withholding discipline they in reality do not truly love that person who has fallen into sin. Jesus has explained to us that after a private attempt to restore a believer from sin and after an attempt with a witness or two, the matter should be taken to the church (Matthew 18:15–17). The reason is this: the main purpose of church discipline is to restore a person into a right relationship with God. This is loving someone. On occasion a church may have to resort to excommunication if the sinner will not repent. At the church in Corinth there was a person who was engaged in sexual activity with his father's wife (1 Corinthians 5:1). Paul chastises the church for not mourning for this person and for not removing him from their midst (5:2).

Your Role in the Church

The exciting truth is that God has called you for a specific role in the local church. A good, healthy perspective on the Christian's part involves the desire to be both ministered to and to minister to others. To drive this point home, the apostle Paul likens the church to a human body in 1 Corinthians 12:12–27. He states that the body is one but that there are many members (vv. 12,14). He then states that every part of the body, though seemingly unimportant, is just as important as the other parts and never acts independently (vv. 15–25). Moreover, if one member of the body suffers, all the other members suffer with it (v. 26). Paul then states, "Now you are Christ's body, and individually members of it" (v. 27).

Interestingly, Paul gives this teaching after he mentions some of the gifts of the Holy Spirit (vv. 1–11). This list is by no means exhaustive. There are more gifts mentioned in Romans 12:6–8; Ephesians 4:11; and 1 Peter 4:11 (see chap. 3 of this book for a list). Peter's words to us should be emblazoned upon our hearts: "As each one has received a special gift, employ it in serving one another, as good stewards of the manifold grace of God" (1 Peter 4:10).

Summary

God acts through the Church for the edification and maturing of believers so that they might worship him more abundantly. The Church is also designed by God to keep us on the right track, on the road of God's will. For this reason, God has instituted church discipline. Finally, you are called to a specific role in God's Church. Christians, using God's gracious gifts, are therefore to use them for service unto one another. In short, don't go to church only to get; go to give as well.

For Discussion

1. What are the two meanings of the word "church"?

2. Why should we go to church?

3. What are the roles of the Church? Can you think of others not mentioned in this chapter?

4. Discuss what you think your special role in the local church is or might be. (Make it a point to pray to the Lord concerning how you might use your gifts to serve the body of Christ.)

5. Discuss how church discipline can be of benefit to the person who has sinned.

 Meditation

What Need We Fear?

That through death He might render powerless him who had the power of death, that is, the devil. (Hebrews 2:14)

Two years ago my wife and I brought a brand-new kitten into our home. We named her "Baklavi" (like the Greek pastry baklava, only with the feminine ending). When spring came, Baklavi was old enough to go outside. And so we let her out during the daylight hours.

Our neighbors also had a cat, a twelve-year veteran of the outdoors named, wouldn't you know it, Spike. Spike was big. He did not take kindly to Baklavi's entrance into his domain. After all, cats have no idea of house lot boundaries.

Baklavi was petrified of Spike. Thankfully, at this point she was able to outrun him—at least most of the time. After two years, our neighbors told us the sad news that Spike (who previously suffered from a cataract, rendering him sightless in one eye) was now totally blind.

However, despite the sad news, and despite the fact that this was *good* news for Baklavi, our cat still remains petrified of Spike. Why? Well, there is no way to communicate to her that

Spike had been rendered virtually powerless. She is still acting as if defeat and harm are as far away as Spike! I am sure that if she knew, she would be victoriously walking around her domain with no fear.

The situation is thankfully much different for Christians. We know that the devil has been rendered powerless because Scripture has told us so. *Therefore* we are not to live our lives as if defeat is imminent. Because of who Christ is and what he has done, we are to have no fear of death and are to consider ourselves victorious through Jesus.

This is the day that the LORD has acted. Rejoice.

We praise you, Lord Jesus, because you are God the Son and because you have acted in our behalf. May our lives, as a result, be one big "therefore." We praise you to the glory of the Father and in the fellowship of the Holy Spirit. Amen.

SUGGESTED READINGS

Christian Apologetics

Paul E. Little. *Know What You Believe*. Wheaton, Ill.: Victor Books, 1970.

Josh McDowell. *Evidence That Demands a Verdict*. San Bernardino, Calif.: Here's Life Publishers, 1979.

Christian Theology

Louis Berkhof. *Systematic Theology*. Grand Rapids, Mich.: Wm. B. Eerdmans Publishing Co., 1941, 1984.

J. Oliver Buswell. *A Systematic Theology of the Christian Religion*. Grand Rapids, Mich.: Zondervan Publishing House, 1962.

Millard J. Erickson. *Christian Theology*. Grand Rapids, Mich.: Baker Book House, 1985.

Donald Guthrie. *New Testament Theology*. Downers Grove, Ill.: InterVarsity Press, 1981.

Charles Hodge. *Systematic Theology*. 3 vols. Grand Rapids, Mich.: Wm. B. Eerdmans Publishing Co., 1986.

George Eldon Ladd. *A Theology of the New Testament*. Grand Rapids, Mich.: Wm. B. Eerdmans Publishing Co., 1974.

Alister E. McGrath. *Christian Theology: An Introduction*. Cambridge, Mass.: Blackwell Publishers, Inc., 1994, 1995, 1996.

GLOSSARY

amillennialism. The view that there is no literal thousand-year earthly reign of Christ (in the senses mentioned in **premillennialism** and **postmillennialism**). Rather, **Christians** have been in the millennium (a thousand years in the figurative sense) since Christ's first coming.

apologetics. The discipline of the defense of the **Christian** faith. The term comes from the Greek word *apologia*, meaning "defense." Christians are called to give reasoned answers for their faith (see 1 Peter 3:15).

Christian. A person who believes in (trusts) the biblical Christ and his sacrificial death on the cross for sin. According to Acts 11:26, the word was coined at Antioch to describe the disciples of Jesus. The term *Christian* is also an adjective, as in Christian **doctrine.**

Christology (krist-*awe*-lo-gee). The study of the **person** and work of Jesus Christ. It deals with who Jesus is and what Jesus has done (and what he presently does).

covenant. A binding agreement between two parties. For our purpose, this is the agreement between God and humanity, which God initiates.

doctrine. Teaching or teachings. **Christian** doctrine then is that which comprises Christianity as a belief structure. There are scores of Christian doctrines—regarding baptism, sacraments, the return of Christ, the Trinity, the resurrection of Christ, the virgin birth, the atonement of Christ, the end times, the ascension of Christ, salvation, the deity and personality of the Holy Spirit, and so on.

eschatology (es-cat-*awe*-lo-gee). Literally "the study of the last things." It deals with topics such as the resurrection of the righteous and the wicked, the second coming of Christ, and heaven.

exegesis (ex-eh-*gee*-sis). Literally "to draw out." Biblical exegesis, then, is the discipline of drawing out the meaning of a text. What the text meant for the biblical writer is the goal of exegesis.

glorification. Pertaining to **Christians,** this generally refers to the resurrected state wherein we shall be given new, immortal, and imperishable bodies.

Godhead. Another term referring to the triune God—the Father, the Son, and the Holy Spirit.

great tribulation. A period of intensified persecution of **Christians** (the Church). *Compare* **midtribulationism, pretribulationism,** and **posttribulationism.**

hermeneutics (her-men-*ooh*-tics). The methodology of bringing exegesis to interpretation. Hermeneutics, then, is the discipline of bringing the original meaning of a text to its present-day application.

incarnate. Literally "in the flesh." In **christological** study, it refers to Jesus when he walked the earth and also to his existence after his resurrection and ascension. The incarnate deity of Christ includes the time of Jesus' conception/birth, continues through his days of walking the earth, and continues presently and into eternity in Christ's resurrected and ascended state.

Incarnation. The event when God the Son took upon himself a full human nature in the womb of the virgin Mary by the Holy Spirit.

inclusivism. The view that salvation includes all religious paths.

interpretation. The application of any given biblical text to the present situation. That is, what any biblical text means to us.

LXX. Numerals denoting the Greek translation of the Hebrew Bible, which is called the Septuagint (the Seventy). LXX is the Roman numeral for seventy. Tradition has it that seventy Hebrew scholars were responsible for the original work. What is fact is that Hebrew scholars (the number is not certain, nor important, for that matter) in the third century B.C. began a translation of the Hebrew Bible into Greek because Greek was replacing Hebrew as the common language in the culture. The LXX has tremendous significance for New Testament studies because it was basically the Bible for most of the New Testament writers. Therefore, in the New Testament are many Old Testament verses quoted from the LXX.

midtribulationism. The view that **Christians** will be subject to only part of the **great tribulation.** Generally in this view the tribulation lasts three and a half years.

modalism. An erroneous view of the **Godhead** that says there is only one **person** in the Godhead, namely the Son. The Son is said to switch "modes" and become the Father at certain times and the Holy Spirit at other times. Another type of modalism states that the Father is the only person in the Godhead. The Father, in turn, becomes the Son or the Holy Spirit at given times in salvation history.

monotheist. A person who believes in the existence of only one God. **Christians** have a monotheistic faith.

orthodoxy. From *orthos,* which means "straight, correct, right," and *doxa,* which means "honor, glory." Orthodox **doctrine,** then, is doctrine or teaching that gives "right honor" to God. When we say that someone is orthodox in the doctrine of the **person** of Christ, we mean that someone is teaching rightly about Christ. In turn, to say that someone espouses "**Christian** orthodoxy" means that the person affirms an essential Christian doctrine (or all the essentials).

person. This English word is derived from the Latin *persona* (pl., *personae*), which the fourth-century theologian Tertullian adopted to describe the members of the **Godhead,** who are biblically and traditionally named the Father, the Son, and the Holy Spirit. When used in relation to the Trinity, the word implies a personal being, one who possesses will, intellect, and emotion and one with whom humanity can enter into personal relationship.

pluralism. The view that the ways of salvation are many.

pneumatology (new-mah-*taw*-lo-gee). The study of the **person** and work of the Holy Spirit; that is, the study of who the Holy Spirit is and what the Holy Spirit has done (and what the Spirit presently does).

postmillennialism. The view that Christ will come back after a millennium of peace and righteousness that is brought about by the preaching of the gospel toward the "Christianizing" of the world.

posttribulationism. The view that Christ will come back *after* the **great tribulation** of **Christians.** Thus, Christians will suffer through the great tribulation.

preexistence. In the study of **Christology,** this refers to the eternal existence of Christ, as the Word (Greek *logos*) before his **incarnation.**

preincarnate. In **christological** study, it refers to Christ's eternal existence before his incarnation. The preincarnate deity of Christ refers to Jesus' preincarnate existence as God the Son.

premillennialism. The view that Christ will come and establish a thousand-year reign of peace and harmony after the **great tribulation.** At this time the millennium will be ushered in, during which Christ will be physically present.

pretribulationism. The view that Christ will come back *before* the **great tribulation.** Thus, **Christians** will not suffer through the great tribulation.

propitiation. In the context of the Atonement, *propitiation* means that the wrath of God was placed upon the substitute (Christ), thereby satisfying the justice of God and removing the wrath of God from those who believe in Christ.

reconciliation. The act in which God brings sinners into fellowship with God's self: "God was in Christ reconciling the world to Himself, not counting their trespasses against them" (2 Corinthians 5:19).

redemption. Literally "to buy back." The buying back, therefore, is associated with payment. In the context of salvation, redemption refers to Christ's redeeming for himself a people with the price of his precious blood. In short, **Christians** have been redeemed by the blood of Christ.

Septuagint (*sep*-tew-ah-jint). *See* **LXX.**

soteriology (so-tear-ree-*awe*-lo-gee). The study of salvation. The main areas of focus are (1) what salvation is and (2) how it is given to humanity.

theology. Technically "the study of God" but also "the study of the things of God" or "the study of the doctrines (teachings) revealed by God in the Bible."

tritheism. An erroneous view of the **Godhead** that says the Trinity consists of three gods. These gods are perceived to be equal in status and, in some theologies, function independently of one another. This inadequate view of the Trinity denies the essential unity of the Godhead, in substance *and* purpose.